from
IDEA
to
PROFIT

from
IDEA

to
PROFIT

how to market innovative products and services

consultant editor: **ADAM JOLLY**

**KOGAN
PAGE**

London and Sterling, VA

Publisher's note

Every possible effort has been made to ensure that the information contained in this book is accurate at the time of going to press, and the publisher and authors cannot accept responsibility for any errors or omissions, however caused. No responsibility for loss or damage occasioned to any person acting, or refraining from action, as a result of the material in this publication can be accepted by the editor, the publisher or any of the authors.

First published in Great Britain and the United States in 2005 by Kogan Page Limited

120 Pentonville Road	22883 Quicksilver Drive
London N1 9JN	Sterling VA 20166-2012
United Kingdom	USA
www.kogan-page.co.uk	

© Kogan Page and Contributors, 2005

ISBN 0 7494 4219 0

British Library Cataloguing-in-Publication Data

A CIP record for this book is available from the British Library.

Library of Congress Cataloging-in-Publication Data

Jolly, Adam.
From idea to profit: how to market innovative products and services/ Adam Jolly.
   p. cm
   ISBN 0-7494-4219-0
   1. New products – Marketing. 2. Strategic planning. I. Title.
HF5415.153.J655 2005
658.8–dc22

                      2004029680

Typeset by Datamatics Technologies Ltd, Mumbai, India
Printed and bound in Great Britain by Clays Ltd, St Ives plc

Contents

v

What makes pricing strategies complex? 31; How should companies address the problem? 32; Conditions for clarity and control 35; Summary 36

Part 1

Innovative strategy

1.1

Breakthroughs in value

*Be an explorer, not a planner, argues John Riker
at Value Innovation Network – Research*

In the 21st century, market competition is more cut-throat and fiercer than ever before, as new technologies, innovative business models and emerging market states in Asia assert themselves in the mainstream of world competitiveness. At the same time, traditional technologies and business models seem to be converging on 'me-too' competition as 'differentiation' becomes an ever-harder game to play. The common response to these pressures is to cut costs and push new products and services aggressively. Yet the medicine is not working. The 'jobless recovery' in the United States, the shift to 'off-shoring' and the ongoing downsizing, rightsizing and restructuring of businesses suggest that a new approach to thinking about competition is needed. Companies cannot save their way to prosperity.

To succeed, companies need to find new ways to grow their business. Their main challenge is to develop business strategies that create new market space by offering their buyers and users compelling value, making their competition irrelevant. 'What separates high-growth companies from the pack is the way managers make sense of how they do business', say Professors W Chan Kim and Renée Mauborgne of INSEAD. They describe these high-growth businesses as Value Innovators, companies that question the implicit assumptions about the conventional logic of strategy.

Most companies develop strategies best described as achieving last year's performance 'plus 10 per cent'. Conventional tools used to develop strategy are applied with immense quantitative rigour only to reduce companies' market horizons. Market share and growth matrices, market attractiveness and relatedness matrices all tend to reduce the market to an absolute number and the company to a relative performer. The challenge for companies is to combine the 'science' of traditional strategy with Value Innovation concepts, frameworks and tools.

According to Kim and Mauborgne, Value Innovators shape industry conditions whereas conventional businesses take them as given. A Value Innovating company does not benchmark competition but rather pursues a quantum leap in value to dominate the market. They target the mass of buyers by focusing on commonalities in what customers value, not on their segmented differences as conventional logic suggests. Conventional businesses determine the products and services they should offer based on the traditional boundaries of their industry, their goal being to maximize the value of those offerings. A Value Innovator thinks in terms of the total solution customers seek even if that takes the company beyond its industry's traditional offerings. These companies formulate strategy to answer the question 'what would we do if we were starting anew?', not just to leverage existing assets and capabilities.

So it seems that how companies approach strategy formulation itself determines their ability to create market space and achieve high growth. Say Kim and Mauborgne, 'Creating new market space requires a different pattern of strategic thinking. Instead of looking within the accepted boundaries that define how we compete, managers can look systematically across them. By doing so, they can find unoccupied territory that represents a real breakthrough in value.'

To identify potential new market space, Value Innovator companies need to rethink the standards of their industry through answering four questions:

- Which industry elements do we take for granted and should we eliminate?
- What elements can we reduce below the industry standard?
- Which elements could we raise well above the industry average?
- Are there new elements that we could create that the industry has never offered?

To create a quantum leap in value companies need to direct all their talent to explore the market. Key to this process is to open up the entire organization to seek growth opportunities. Most companies sit on a goldmine of talented and capable people, yet few tap into them in developing strategy. By bringing together a diverse team of employees from across functions, levels and geographies where appropriate, an organization can foster new ways of thinking and a wider business perspective.

Strategy needs to become more of a visual and intuitive process than purely numeric and analytic. Strategy formulation needs to consider both a company's traditional market as well as all alternative markets. Until you expand your definition of your market you will not be able to expand the possibilities of your market offer. Filling up your petrol tank is somehow similar to filling up your wallet at an ATM. Using sophisticated software to write and calculate can still be achieved with a pencil. Going to the mall will always be an option for those who shop on the internet. Driving to your destination is a viable alternative to flying.

Through this qualitative process of market exploration, companies can begin to look at their industry and business through a new set of lenses. They learn about their customers' dreams and hates, their aspirations and irritations. From these insights, Value Innovators begin to prospect for widely shared customer perspectives from which they identify potential growth markets. Even more important than exploring current buyers and users is to probe non-buyers and non-users why they are not in the market. This rich image of the wider market translates into breakthrough ideas for new market space.

By opening up strategy formulation to a company's entire organization and by applying a wide-angle lens to their thinking, a business can create new market space. It requires immense leadership and courage to abandon the ritual comfort of traditional strategy development and to embark on this process. But given the unrelenting pressure of competition, the need to introduce unconventional thinking will become more of an imperative for all companies seeking to create successful growth strategies.

For all companies and all industries the main challenge will be to develop business strategies that map new market space. Strategy formulation will be more akin to exploring than planning. As explorers, the winning companies will learn to identify, architect and exploit new market space. As planners, the losing ones will continue to believe that their industry standards are predictable and that by gaining a few more market share points they will remain 'competitive'. By continually creating new market space companies can offer their employees, customers and shareholders long-term growth and value.

John Riker: johnlriker@aol.com

Market-led innovation

Customer preferences are as important in creating points of difference as new product development, argues Peter Soddy at The Innovators Club

Innovation is fast becoming one of the most overused words by those who make the most noise but appear to understand it least. It is moving inexorably towards the vocab' graveyard which is littered with the likes of 'best practice', 'empowerment', 'people make the difference' and many other such flavour-of-the-month statements which *appear* to have come and gone having made no real impact upon the business universe.

However, if business managers do not seriously consider how they might become more innovative in their approach to gaining a competitive edge in their marketplace and securing a modicum of long-term sustainability for their business then they will be 'basket cases' alongside the redundant vocab'.

All of the above are in fact essentially 'good things' that we should all be doing in our businesses but the day-to-day problems faced by those of us involved in keeping the business alive and kicking tend to outweigh the 'good things' and hence, the longer-term thinking.

The reason for the low uptake of these 'good things' originates because, as owners and operators of smaller and medium-sized companies, we need to have answers to the simplistic, 'so what' questions.

Generally speaking, the people responsible for starting and running these businesses are motivated by the belief that they can earn a better standard of living or quality of life for their families by following this route rather than being an employee. When a new proposal or concept is put before us we first evaluate it on its merits with regard to *'how will this help me achieve my objective for running the business?'* In other words, *'So what's that got to do with my business and what difference will it make?'*

I believe a key reason for the apparent low uptake of 'innovation' in business is because the real benefits are not properly presented to the owners and managers of small and medium-sized companies. The communications on this topic support the impression that it is all to do with invention, R&D, new product development and requiring big budget commitments, which are at risk if the 'eureka' moment does not occur.

For around 10 years, since the formation of the 'Innovation Unit', the DTI have promoted innovation as the 'exploitation of good ideas'. A more accurate and meaningful definition which attempts to address the *'so what?'* and *'why bother?'* questions is that market-led innovation is: 'the exploitation of good ideas which win and sustain a customer preference'.

This addresses the conjunction of marketing, innovation and best practice. The linkage between innovation and customer preference, and hence business performance, in this definition provides a clear answer to the questions above.

In practical terms, market-led innovation is a carefully coordinated and regularized planning process involving a wide cross-section of views and actions from employees in bringing about superior added value for customers. From this process, competitive advantage and increased profitability for the company are derived.

The rationale behind The Innovators Club (and that of The Enterprise Network when we first authored that programme back in 1987 before it was adopted by *The Sunday Times*) is that innovation should only be market-led. Equally, it should be applied to every aspect of the business, 'above and below' the line.

I believe that innovation applied to improving an internal process, which may be invisible to the customer, is just as valid as the development of a new product. If the strict focus on innovation being 'market-led' is maintained, the new or improved process will inevitably result in a customer advantage or point of difference for your company in the marketplace.

Maybe it will result in my ability to deliver products quicker than you and hence, be perceived by the customer as an advantage of dealing with my company when there is little to choose between our products or services or their pricing.

Following this simplistic example for a moment, let us suppose that if I can now process orders more quickly it means that I can also process more orders in the working day and improve my sales throughput, opportunities for incremental revenue, revenue per employee, stock turn rates etc.

The answers to the '*So what?*' and '*Why bother?*' questions in this case soon become apparent when the concept and benefits of innovation are explained from the customer's point of view. And at this time I am regarding UK business managers as the customer as it is they who have to be convinced and accept that there are advantages in making changes to the way in which they currently operate. We are not talking about change for change sake but change for improved business and profitability sake.

OK, so this may be stating the obvious but if it is, how come that innovation awards always seem to be granted to those companies that have come up with the best new product or maybe their use of e-business. They very rarely seem to look inside the organization or at the heart of the business.

A great proportion of running a business can be put down to common sense but I believe in the old adage that success and differentiation come from identifying the sense before it becomes common. Think of the business as a flowering plant, with the blooms and scent being that which attracts the customers to your fold. Then consider the same flowering plant with no roots and nothing below the soil line – now how long will the blooms last?

For a business to bloom it must have healthy roots otherwise the blooms will die, unless of course they are false blooms, in which case the customer will soon suss that out! The roots may be labelled as 'Cost Control', 'Supply Chain Management', 'Business Process Efficiencies', 'Market and Competitor Knowledge' and many others.

The first step is to identify and label the roots that drive the growth of your business, and then to decide which to tackle first. These are more commonly referred to as Critical Success Factors but they should be viewed from the market perspective and you should tackle those that will create the biggest difference in the marketplace as the first priority.

It is often accepted that something must be done to improve efficiencies and profitability but the problem comes with knowing where to start. The home page of The Innovators Club website – www.theinnovatorsclub.co.uk – carries a link labelled 'The Health Check Zone'. This contains two quick health check tools which companies can follow.

The first is a modified version of the DTI's 'Living Innovation' programme and the second is a check, which is based on the Winning Report. This has been developed by us to provide a quick diagnostic tool and to indicate a possible start point for the innovation process within the business.

Real value comes when these are used as the basis for internal discussions to decide the areas where changes can be made and the priority to be applied to each aspect.

When you have conducted the health check for yourself, ask your colleagues to go through the same process and then compare the results. The debate about the differences will be most valuable and tell you something about varying internal perceptions about the business.

The health checks are quick indicators and not intended to be online consultancy but they do provide a useful guide. The outcome of the diagnostic tools is a brief menu of practical actions which businesses can pursue to address the areas of need highlighted in the test results. It is not another signposting tool that sends you around the websites of the world without ever actually providing any real help or guidance.

Market-led innovation in business will come from anywhere and everywhere in the organization. It is not just about invention but it certainly will include invention and an inventive approach to overcoming the problems of the day or the gaining of a competitive advantage for the future. To coin a phrase 'borrowed' from a recent TV commercial for an airline: *'When was the last time you did something for the first time?'*

An Innovators Club supplement in *The Sunday Telegraph* featured a head-to-head interview with Trevor Bayliss, the renowned creator of the clockwork radio and self-confessed mad inventor, and Sir John Harvey-Jones, the former ICI chairman, business guru and presenter of the *Trouble-Shooter* series. The interview revealed that, despite their distinctly different approaches, they have a common bond in how business is driven forward.

In Trevor's words, 'People like me couldn't achieve what we do without businessmen like him.' In other words, successful businesses are taken to market and driven by a balanced mix of 'mad inventors', tempered by business people with a firm controlling hand on the processes while retaining a market focus.

In order to improve internal processes you must involve a cross-section of the people working in those processes. Clearly, they will know all the niggles with the current system and where improvements and efficiency gains are readily available.

If you do that and seek input from a suitable team then you are starting to see the real benefits of following some of the concepts mentioned and apparently dismissed earlier. For example:

■ you are now starting to pursue *best practices;*

- you are now starting to *empower* people in the business to make a difference; and

- you are demonstrating that, in your business, *people really do make the difference*.

So, *what* is innovation about?

Market-led innovation must be about creating a profitable difference with long-term sustainability for your business in the marketplace. If you don't think you can make a difference then don't do it, but go back and have another look because you've probably missed something along the way.

Peter Soddy is managing director of Potential Development Ltd and co-founder of The Sunday Times Enterprise Network and The Innovators Club. Further information: peter@potential.co.uk

1.3

Outsmarting the competition

A new type of company is emerging, says Chris McDonald, planning director of BDH\TBWA since 2001. One that is ideas-driven

THE COMMERCIAL VALUE OF IDEAS

If you are reading this book, it is fair to assume that you have the ability to generate 'ideas'. This is a skill that is often undervalued within business. The ability to think creatively is considered a 'soft' skill, in contrast to the rational, and arguably more accountable, areas such as production, structure and finance. A 10 per cent improvement in production efficiency produces an immediate effect on the bottom line, but the value of a new way of thinking is difficult to quantify.

However, there are indications that we are now in the middle of a fundamental change in what is required to run a successful business. Thirty years ago, the most successful companies were likely to have a product with a sustainable advantage over its direct competitors – something marketers liked to call its USP (unique selling proposition).

As the level of competition increased, the likelihood of having a sustainable product advantage was significantly reduced. The battle shifted from market growth to market share and companies devoted more time to understanding what their competitors were up to. As a result, product improvements were copied in a matter of weeks rather than years. It is now common practice for larger companies to gather intelligence on a competitive launch and introduce spoiling tactics before the new product is even on the shelf. This strategy is often used in the publishing industry where magazines and newspapers are frequently launched purely to undermine a new competitive title.

The waning power of the 'USP' fuelled the growth of the 'service culture' and this next wave of marketing is still largely prevalent. As the rational differences between products were reduced, the most successful companies became those who could demonstrate a better understanding of their customers and were more responsive to their needs. This still holds true.

However, the past decade has also seen the emergence of a new type of company: those that are *idea-driven*. These companies still produce best-in-class products and tend to be at the leading edge of customer service, but they also have a commitment to creating value through bringing something new to the market.

Think about those companies we tend to use as a benchmark: Virgin, easyJet, Prêt à Manger, Dyson. All brought a new way of thinking to an established market.

The market leaders have gone from being product-led to service-led to ideas-driven. And these idea-driven companies are more profitable.

A recent study by the *Financial Times* revealed that, of 100 new business launches, 86 per cent were 'me-toos' or offered only incremental improvements. These generated 62 per cent of launch revenues and 39 per cent of profits. In contrast, the remaining 14 per cent – those that created new markets or redefined existing ones – generated 38 per cent of revenues and over 60 per cent of the profit.

However, while this is good news for those of us who see ourselves in the 'ideas' business, the ability to generate ideas is no more likely to create commercial success than the ability to produce a profit and loss account.

Success depends on understanding the difference between the traditional and commercial definition of an idea – and having a framework for consistently differentiating between the two.

COMMERCIAL IDEAS: A NEW DEFINITION

The dictionary definition of an idea is 'a conception or plan formed by mental effort': this is the area we are most comfortable with. We have what we *believe* to be an original piece of thinking, but have no way of evaluating it beyond our own experience.

Is the idea as original as we believe it is? In what way is it different to what already exists? Is this difference sufficiently motivating to a large enough number of people? How much would they be willing to pay? Once someone has copied the idea, where do we go next?

I have a simple way of defining an idea which has the potential for commercial success. A commercially sound idea should be capable of:

- producing a step-change in consumer attitudes or behaviour;
- providing a long-term focus for the company;
- forcing competitors to rethink.

The basis of this simple framework is that a commercial idea has to be competitive. And to be competitive, an idea has to bring something to the market that challenges existing behaviour and significantly changes this in our favour. An idea is unlikely to be a commercial success if it simply accepts the rules established by the current players.

Similarly, a good question to ask is 'how will our competitors react?' If you feel your competitors are unlikely to respond, the chances are you haven't hurt them enough and the idea is unlikely to shake up the market.

Equally, I have seen many ideas lost because they appear completely to contradict accepted wisdom. It is easy to become nervous and lose confidence in an idea because the *current* market leaders seem to see the world a different way. But these are often the most powerful ideas. Before the arrival of Southwest Airlines or easyJet, it was unthinkable that a market-leading airline would compete on anything other than the comfort of the in-flight experience.

If you start to get nervous about how radical an idea might appear, ask yourself how you would feel if your competitor did this. A good idea will have the potential to frighten you.

The focus on producing a long-term direction for the company is designed to ensure that this is more than a transient idea. Even if it can be patented, it is safe to assume that, once the patent runs out, a successful idea will be copied. Short-term, we should assume that someone is already working on a similar – if not better – development. Assuming the product innovation is copied, what is there about the *way* we will bring this to market that gives us a sustainable competitive advantage beyond the product improvement itself?

This could mean using marketing to 'own' the idea – in the minds of both the trade and the consumer (despite the fact that most manufacturers now produce bagless vacuum cleaners in the UK, this is intrinsically associated with Dyson); finding a new route to market (Dell); having a distinct attitude, which is difficult for the competition to copy (Apple); or having an ongoing programme of development (Sony).

A CONVENTIONS-DRIVEN APPROACH TO COMPETITIVE ANALYSIS

As the level of competition has increased, most companies have developed regular systems for evaluating competitive activity. However, this is often left to the most junior person within the marketing department and is treated as a factual report rather than an opportunity to think behind the observations (the 'what') and identify any underlying competitive trends (the 'why'). This can frequently provide the platform for market-changing ideas, but is an area that is frequently overlooked.

Rather than simply commenting on competitive activity, I find it useful to pull this together into what we call market 'conventions'. These conventions can be grouped into categories that are most useful for each particular market. Typically this would include 'corporate conventions', 'marketing conventions', 'communication conventions' and 'consumer conventions'.

Most markets seem to work within conventions that are followed by the vast majority of competitors. Corporate mission statements will be similar, advertising may follow a predictable structure, or all competitors may be targeting the same people in the same way. If you are looking to introduce a commercially successful idea, the chances are that your idea needs to break at least one – if not more – of these conventions.

In particular, the real insight comes from trying to identify the underlying assumption that drives these market conventions. This is the central belief that underpins the current market dynamic. If it can be challenged, this will completely change the rules of the market and open up potentially profitable new market space.

Conventions analysis can provide a framework for evaluating existing ideas, or be used to generate new ideas which challenge market assumptions.

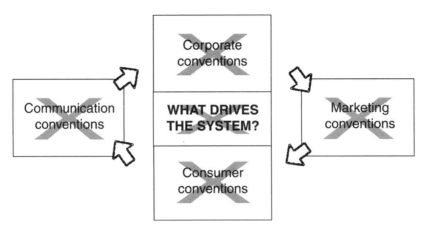

Figure 1.3 (i)   *Identifying conventions*

MARKET SPACE VS MARKET SHARE

One of the most frequent mistakes I have seen in evaluating the commercial potential for an idea is an obsession with market share and, in particular, a limited focus on *current* competitors. This accepts the current definition of the market and fails to take account of any more radical change.

Who would have predicted Virgin's expansion from a record company to an international airline? Or PlayStation's transformation of childish computer games into a legitimate adult pastime?

Commercial history is littered with the remains of companies that failed to see that the nature of their business was changing. Equally, most of today's successful companies have redefined markets rather than try to establish a competitive advantage within a framework defined to suit someone else.

Within my company, we prefer to evaluate an idea on its potential to create a larger share of the future rather than simply increase market share. This encourages us to think beyond existing structures, anticipate new competitors and create new market space.

EVALUATING THE IDEA

Just because an idea is competitive, there is no guarantee that it will be successful. Many other factors come into play, most of which are covered elsewhere in this book.

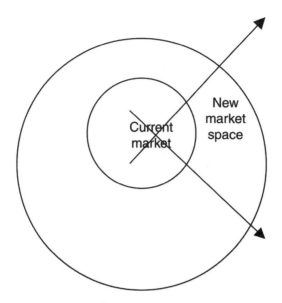

Figure 1.3 (ii) *Creating a larger share of the future*

However, it is still amazing how many ideas are taken to market without the most basic form of evaluation. Ultimately, consumer and trade research are necessary to help evaluate the true potential of the idea. But this often requires a serious commitment in terms of time and money.

In particular, once an idea is exposed to the trade, there is every possibility that competitors will become aware of it and – unless you can be sure of confidentiality, or the idea is patented – this is best delayed as long as possible.

Before commissioning what could be an expensive piece of research, I would recommend a very simple approach to evaluating initial ideas. This will not replace more specific consumer research, but will help to screen out those ideas which have real potential from those that don't. We call this the 'idea integrity check'.

This simple model is based on the premise that to have a chance of commercial success, an idea must be:

■ true to the values of the company behind it;
■ different to what is already available from the competition;
■ relevant and motivating to the consumer.

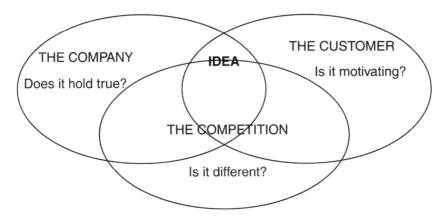

Figure 1.3 (iii)   *Idea integrity check*

Some initial consumer research may still be required to answer the third question although, at this screening stage, this could be conducted on a relatively small scale. In particular, if budgets don't initially allow for a significant piece of external consumer research, don't underestimate the value of exposing an idea to a few relevant friends, or conducting some internal research within the company. The conventions analysis will help to identify the degree of competitive differentiation.

CHECKLIST: OUTSMARTING THE COMPETITION

- Is your idea strong enough to:
  - produce a step-change in consumer attitudes or behaviour?
  - force competitors to rethink?
  - provide a long-term focus for the company?
- How will your competitors react?
- How would you feel if your competitor introduced this idea first?
- What steps have you taken to ensure continued success once any initial product advantage disappears?
- What are the conventions that currently define your market?
- What is the underlying assumption behind these conventions?
- In what way does/could your idea challenge them?

- Think beyond existing competitors. The most profitable ideas create new market space rather than increase market share.

- Apply a simple evaluation criteria to the idea before commissioning more expensive consumer or trade research.

Former planning director of HHCL and head of planning at Chiat/Day Toronto, Chris McDonald has spent almost 20 years in the advertising industry, working with clients from Nissan to Microsoft. He has been planning director of BDH\TBWA since 2001.

1.4

Designing better customer experiences

Why is innovation such a struggle for so many organizations,
asks Jane Pritchard of IDEO

In today's highly competitive and fast-changing marketplace, everything is subject to innovation – physical objects, financial services, political and social systems, medical research and even health care services.

Generally it is not a shortage of ideas that prevents organizations from becoming more innovative but rather the confusion as to what innovation means and what steps need to be taken in order to create a more innovative organization.

Many organizations find being innovative difficult for a variety of reasons. One reason is that people have very different perceptions of the meaning of innovation – even within the same organization. For example, innovation likely means something very different to a marketing director than it does to an R&D director. There is often a lack of common understanding and language around innovation within an organizational context.

Another thing to acknowledge is that having good ideas can be easy but actually getting them to market is a different matter. Ideas need to be turned into actionable plans – whether they are for new products, services, systems or customer experiences. However, this exercise requires lots of hard work as well as the right mix of people, skills, capabilities and organizational structure.

Companies need to remember to nurture and build their innovation capabilities, which includes increasing their ability to learn, and continually renew themselves – sometimes incrementally and other times radically.

So, how can companies aim to be continuously innovative and thus increase revenues? Well, applying a systematic design and innovation process can be a powerful way to innovate across a variety of industries. This 'innovation process' can be leveraged across product, service, system or environment design.

FIVE STEPS IN THE PROCESS OF DESIGNING BETTER CUSTOMER EXPERIENCES

IDEO's human-centred innovation methodology has five basic steps that are interpreted differently for each project according to its nature.

Observation

Cognitive psychologists, anthropologists, sociologists and designers team up to observe real people in real-life situations to find out what makes them tick: what confuses them, what they like, what they hate, if they have latent needs not addressed by current products and services. We want to understand the entire customer experience.

Brainstorming

Once we've gathered data during our observations, we analyse it, create brainstorm topics, and begin an intensive idea-generating session. Such sessions usually last about an hour. We have a list of 'brainstorm rules' that the team will follow:

- Defer judgement.
- Build on the ideas of others.
- Encourage wild ideas.
- Go for quantity.
- Be visual.
- Stay focused on the topic.
- One conversation at a time.

Rapid prototyping and visualizing

This step involves creating mock-ups and models – these may take the form of a physical working model, a computer-based rendering or a short film or video which portrays life with a future product, service or system before it even exists. For new product categories the customer experience is sometimes visualized using composite characters and storyboard-illustrated scenarios.

Evaluating and refining

It is important to engage the client actively in this step as we begin to narrow down our ideas and make choices. We try not to get too attached to the first few prototypes, because we know they'll change. No idea is so good that it cannot be improved upon. Our teams seek input from a variety of stakeholders, including knowledgeable people not directly involved with the project. We look for what works and what doesn't and we incrementally improve the product in the next round.

Implementation

This phase is often the longest and technically most challenging in the development process, but the ability to implement successfully lends credibility to the creative work that goes before. At this stage we draw upon our capabilities in engineering, design and social sciences.

Translating ideas into actionable plans often requires that companies build innovation capability within their own organizations. Over the years, many of our clients have asked us not only to develop products, services and environments for them but also to help them build innovation practices and capability within their own organizations.

In response to this market need, we began to collaborate with our clients through intensive workshops and programmes where we focus on sharing our innovation practices by immersing our clients in a process of 'learn by doing'.

These types of workshop engagements generally have two key aims:

- To generate a landscape of new ideas together that addresses an organization's specific needs. For example, during a three-day workshop we will conduct observations and generate hundreds of ideas through brainstorming sessions. Such collaboration will enable us to prototype some ideas quickly with the goal of communicating them to a larger audience within our client's organization.

■ Secondly, by engaging in a different way of working, participants from the client organization will take on board some of the creative behaviours and techniques that IDEO uses in its own work. Workshop participants are equipped with new innovation practices and methods which they can use to further develop innovation capability within their own organization on both an individual level and a team level. Workshop participants become a catalyst for developing an innovation capability.

THREE TIPS TO REMEMBER!

1. *Go for quantity.* Aim for as many new ideas as possible. The key is to have lots of ideas – out of thousands of ideas you might get a hundred experiments from which ten projects might emerge and finally out of all of this – one may be a winner!

2. *Create interdisciplinary teams.* At IDEO, teams are composed of people from a broad range of disciplines, including cognitive psychology, industrial design, interaction design and different kinds of engineering as well as management consulting. It is also quite common to find ourselves working alongside employees from other offices or on projects staffed at different IDEO locations. This fluidity ensures that ideas have a chance to propagate through our organization and that creativity within IDEO remains stimulated through the continual injection of new influences.

3. *Collaborate radically.* Radical collaboration attempts to break through normal client–vendor communication barriers by structuring a programme where the client and vendor exist as a unified team. Through this effort we ensure a higher level of teamwork, shared ownership and participation, which we believe ultimately result in the best programmes. Many of our clients set up 'camp' at IDEO for extended periods of time.

SUMMARY

IDEO's five-step process is a powerful engine for innovation and can be widely applied and used for new-to-the-world products, for financial services or even for designing the patient experience in a hospital. It places users, or customers, in the centre to ensure that the technologies employed serve their purpose.

It is a process that can be used by business practitioners, designers and engineers alike, which encourages radical collaboration in multidisciplinary teams and can be transferred into an organization at all levels.

Jane Pritchard is Head of the Transformation practice for IDEO in Europe. She leads a variety of Innovation services, including IDEO U's, Innovation Audits and design transformation projects. She holds a BA in Interior Design from Ryerson University, Toronto, Canada and a Masters in Design Strategy and Innovation from Brunel University, UK.

IDEO is an international design and innovation company located in the United States and Europe. It provides service, environment and product design for clients worldwide, creating tangible strategies for innovation. Its clients include Braun, Diageo, LEGO, Nestlè, BBC, P&G and Vodafone. Further information: Tel: +44 (0)20 7713 2600; www.ideo.com.

1.5

Value propositions

Take research and development to your customers as soon as you can, says Peter White, Chairman of YTKO Cambridge, and get them to set price and performance expectations

Innovation needs marketing, and vice versa. 'The business enterprise has two – and only two – basic functions: marketing and innovation. Marketing and innovation produce results; all the rest are costs.' So said business guru Peter Drucker. He said it in 1953, and we're only now putting the two together and getting the rewards we deserve. We have to market our innovation hard. Make it attractive. Grab attention. Position it as the killer application or the must-have. And then?

Shouting about innovation still doesn't get you the sales. You must show the inherent value in your offering. If it's not obvious, then get your customers to work with you to make it visible value.

Taking the time to do a quick value proposition, even before your idea has gelled, not only shows you what the real worth of your innovation is, but also indicates how – and to whom – the concept should be marketed.

A value proposition attempts to project potential quantified benefits to a prospective user; benefits they hope to receive through the implementation of your offering. You can kick-start the whole, essential, business development process by demonstrating to the prospect that you are concerned with meeting their needs and requirements. You prove that your offering has value in their situation.

A value proposition isn't simply a sum showing how many times faster, or cheaper, your offering is. It takes into account how much your solution costs to buy, implement, and maintain, and then details what the savings, or advantages, are. One caveat: value propositions work really well when you're selling business-to-business. If you're in the consumer marketplace, then you'll need good market research to give you a clear idea of the value your customers will put on intangibles such as status and fashion – even on innovation itself.

Let's be specific: the four steps here should be enough for any company, large or small, to determine whether its newest concept will sell:

1. Start off by describing what the prospect could improve – such as productivity, efficiency, revenues, safety, time to market; what they may reduce – costs, staff turnover; and what they might create – new product to market – by buying from you.

2. Then project how much this improvement would be worth in terms of cash, reduced timescales or provide a percentage/range. You'll need to have done your homework on what the typical costs of people, materials and machinery are. But of course you are talking to the market regularly, and you're not doing your innovation in a vacuum, are you?

3. Now you'll be able to talk to your prospective users about what they'll be able to do differently. Here you can create a scenario of a wonderful, innovative future.

    And, at this time, any interested customer will ask you straight out: what will it cost me?

4. Don't tell them. Get them to agree on what the saving really could be, or the extra productivity. Be specific, but keep it experimental and informal. And ask them what proportion of that likely saving they'd be prepared to pay. Using this value proposition play, you set the scene, you and the customer jointly set the value, and the customer sets the price.

If you can't make it for what they'll pay, you've saved yourself development headaches, and the pain of trying to sell an unwanted product. It's back to the drawing board, but better informed, and with a clear cost target.

At the very least, communicating your outline value proposition – and showing how you arrived at the worth of your solution – will create curiosity in the mind of the client. They will want to know if it really will apply in their own situation, and will work with you to help develop the best solution.

Then do it all over again. And again. You can never have too much market information.

All of this is common sense. Like much of marketing, it's obvious and sensible. Yet very few of the many SMEs we see have really talked about the customer's needs and processes. 'We send our business development manager out three times a week to talk to customers', said one founder. 'We're building a terrific sales pipeline.' To most of those prospective purchasers, the new product would indeed be suitable. But none of them had talked about value, and none about the return on investment they would like to see if they went for this particular innovation.

Companies get overly secretive. 'If we talk to the market now, then our competitors will pick up what we're doing and we'll lose our edge.' We riposted: if you reckon your competition is so good that they can catch up with your R&D in a few weeks, are you really innovating?

Let's agree, then, that every innovative company needs to engage with the customer at the earliest opportunity. A market is not just a single buyer, though. Even within the customer there are different roles, and different value judgements, which you must assess and then address.

The buyer determines needs, assesses suppliers, orders and pays for and takes delivery of a product or service. The value proposition to the buyer often focuses on speed of delivery, quality of service, maintenance levels, service level agreements and overall quality delivery.

The user motivation is different. They want to do their job better. These are people who are looking for an outcome. It may be doing a job that they haven't previously been able to do, or simply performing that job better, or removing obstacles in their way. This is the group focused on the performance, and the value proposition for the user needs to reflect these outcomes.

This is early-stage marketing. It sits neatly alongside your early-stage innovation, and informs those concepts and creativity. It ensures there's no 'ivory tower' of invention, and provides a reality – and profitability – check, so you know you've got a business to back your innovation. And it adds new resources to your innovation team: people who daily struggle with the problems you're looking to solve, and who will tell you exactly the value of what you're working on. They'll do that for free, and then pay you money when you can prove your concept to them. Get engaged.

Peter White works closely with scientists and technologists to create and develop innovative and sustainable market-driven enterprises funded from venture and private capital. Chairman of YTKO, he is a leading practitioner of enterprise prototyping, an innovative YTKO process to gain market feedback, awareness and early revenues for fast-growth organizations seeking to exploit innovation. He consults with many investors, and regularly reports on future trends, market dynamics and venture opportunities for companies in the UK and United States.

Peter is a regular participant in workshops and conferences, presenting on market strategy, value creation, innovation exploitation and enterprise development. He is responsible for developing the YTKO Incubator in Cambridge, which has helped create and sustain over 50 jobs, and a second incubator launched in Norwich.

He sits on the board of three start-ups, is a mentor and teaching member of the University of Cambridge Entrepreneurship Centre, an Honorary Alumnus of the Theseus Management Institute, Sophia Antipolis, France, an elected member of the Marketing Society, and Director of Bioscience Yorkshire Enterprise Fellowships.

Further details: www.ytko.com

1.6

Pricing: the bigger picture

Pricing was never simple, but is becoming more complex,
says Malcolm McKenzie, a Partner in the RSM Robson
Rhodes Business Consulting group

I can get you turnover any time, we simply cut the prices; I can get you profit any-
time, we simply put the prices up; the real strategic issue is to get the balance right
to attract and retain customers long-term. (Former Deputy Chairman of a leading
UK retailer)

It is doubtful that managing prices was ever that simple, although the company concerned was highly successful for a number of decades. However,
pricing strategy is now much more complex. The questions are why, and
what are the keys to effective management?

WHAT MAKES PRICING STRATEGIES COMPLEX?

There are four main drivers of complexity in the development and management of pan-European pricing strategies:

1. *The growth of pan-European (and global) retailers and manufacturers*: This gives rise to cross-border trading or the 'grey market'. More painful for manufacturers is the rise of retailers who use their knowledge of prices in different countries to demand the 'lowest' price everywhere.

2. *EU anti-competition legislation*: Companies have to ensure that their terms and conditions do not infringe any EU competition rules. Otherwise, they risk potential fines of up to 10 per cent of their worldwide turnover. Companies recently found guilty of infringements include AstraZeneca and others for being in a pharmaceutical cartel, and Ryanair for getting 'illegal' discounts from Charleroi airport. Microsoft appears to be next in the frame – just think what 10 per cent of their revenues would mean, if found guilty.

3. *The internet*: This has made transparency of prices across the globe far greater. It has also increased the likelihood of customers shopping around or becoming tougher in their negotiations based on better knowledge.

4. *Two critical internal business attributes*: How actively the company manages the pricing issue; and how well it uses its information to develop, manage and control coherent (pan-European) pricing strategies.

HOW SHOULD COMPANIES ADDRESS THE PROBLEM?

There are three basic questions you need to answer:

- How active are you/should you be in managing pricing strategy?
- What information is vital for you to establish a coherent and defensible pricing strategy?
- Where and how should you set the strategic pricing level?

How active should companies be?

It is an axiom that pricing strategy is a dynamic process. You cannot decide it and leave it. The history of grocery retailing in the UK at least shows that if manufacturers do not actively manage their pricing strategies, then retailers will quickly move from subservience to dominance.

There is no other answer – companies have to manage their pricing strategies continuously and actively.

How active is your company?

This table shows our basic framework for assessing the level of price management in a company.

Table 1.6 (i)　Framework for assessing price management

	Reactive management	Semi-active management	Active management
Customer relationship	▪ Avoids customer discussions ▪ Trade negotiations based on price not performance ▪ Confrontational approach	▪ Trade negotiations based on price not performance	▪ Rewards and discounts encourage cooperation ▪ Customer negotiations across Europe based on market development and cost efficiency
Pricing management	▪ No multi-market price responsibility	▪ Clear responsibilities for international accounts ▪ Defence strategy in place	▪ International account teams with appropriate skills and systems ▪ Multi-market pricing strategy team
Coordination of prices	▪ Little price coordination between countries	▪ Management understands multi-market pricing issues ▪ Loose coordination of prices between countries	▪ Good coordination of multi-market pricing information
Insight into pricing issues	▪ Little/poor understanding of multi-market pricing issues/implications ▪ Poor information on discount terms/structure within key accounts ▪ Reliance on customers to provide multi-market pricing information	▪ Coordination of pricing information across markets/accounts	▪ Multi-market perspective on business by senior/key account managers

What information is vital?

Most companies have a basic price list from which they give discounts to 'favoured' customers. The aim is, or should be, to convince customers to buy their products or services in preference to those offered by the competition.

Yet, it is surprising how many companies cannot identify the scope and scale of the discounts that they offer their customers. Nor can many compare the discounts given to pan-European customers in the different operating countries.

This gives rise to two pricing issues:

- 'If you can't measure it...': Lack of relevant, accurate, and timely information will hinder any attempt to develop a coherent pricing strategy.
- The basic tenet of EU law is that discounts must be open to all: If you cannot justify your discounts and pricing strategy, then you dramatically increase your risk of infringing EU law.

EU law – the principles of compliance

Within the framework of EU law, there are three principal information requirements:

1. Use common terminology in your business to describe trading terms and discounts. Figure 1.6(i) illustrates this.
2. Understand the true cost of serving your customer base. This involves:
   - detailed knowledge of the transparent or tangible costs, and
   - the allocation of the non-tangible costs to areas such as the sales force, promotions, logistics, servicing and administration, order processing, and the cost of credit.
3. Develop trading terms based on defensible conditions. For example, you can only defend volume-related discounts if there is an underlying reason supporting them. Giving a discount simply because someone buys more from you would infringe EU law. However, you can justify such discounts if you base them on reducing delivery and administration costs (eg bulk shipment of goods reduces handling, paperwork, and warehousing costs, etc).

Where should strategic pricing levels be set?

The answer varies for every company. Amongst other things, it depends on:

- having accurate facts and figures;

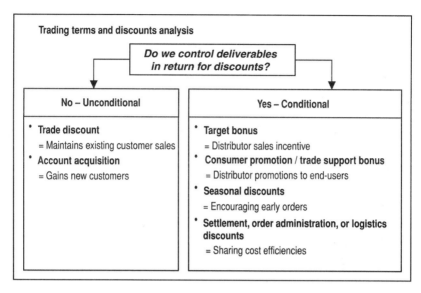

Figure 1.6 (i) *Trading terms and discounts analysis*

- knowing the market environment;
- understanding the corporate goals that the pricing strategy is designed to deliver.

More generally, most practitioners advocate monitoring customers' pricing levels within a series of 'price corridors' (Figure 1.6(ii) illustrates this idea).

CONDITIONS FOR CLARITY AND CONTROL

However, you can achieve a more sophisticated solution provided you fully adopt the principle of conditional discounts. You can then structure discounts to achieve the right balance between the contribution and the investment. Figure 1.6(iii) graphically illustrates the result: customer B makes a lower net contribution than customer A, but, because it cannot meet the required conditions, does not get such a high volume discount, or any range discount.

The strategic debate, when applying the conditional approach, focuses on the true value of the customers to the achievement of corporate goals. Nevertheless, adopting it requires robust facts, based on an assessment of the cost of service, and the analysis of the effect of different discount levels. This leads straight back to the issues of active management and vital information.

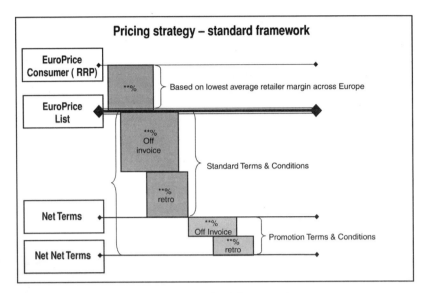

Figure 1.6 (ii)   *Pricing strategy – standard framework*

SUMMARY

Lord Leverhulme is famously quoted as saying, 'I know half of my advertising works, but unfortunately I do not know which half.'

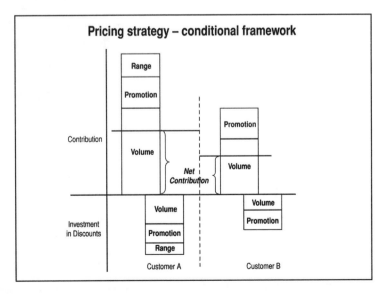

Figure 1.6 (iii)   *Pricing strategy – conditional framework*

Companies that allow this view to apply to their sales will lose out to their better-informed competitors. Knowing half the effect of your price discounts only guarantees forcing your pricing strategy into a reactive response to market conditions and competitor activity. Companies that want to develop and manage effective pricing strategies must be able to see the whole picture.

Malcolm McKenzie is a Partner in the RSM Robson Rhodes Business Consulting group. If you would like to discuss the ideas or charts in this article or any other pricing issues in more detail, please contact Malcolm on 020 7865 2875 or at malcolm.mckenzie@rsmi.co.uk.

Intellectual property

*Don't neglect your intellectual property and allow
your creativity to be exploited by someone else,
says Lawrence Smith-Higgins of the UK Patent Office*

Every business uses intellectual property (IP); it could be in the name it trades under, the processes it uses or the products and services it provides. IP is an asset, but unlike most other assets it is more likely to have been neglected because IP is not easy to identify and value. IP is becoming an increasingly important part of our daily lives. Businesses must be in a position to make informed decisions about protecting the IP they create.

WHY INTELLECTUAL PROPERTY?

The system of IP rights can be used to safeguard your competitive edge and give added value to a business idea. In what is increasingly a knowledge-driven economy, IP is becoming a key consideration in day-to-day business decisions, not just as an asset but also as a means of increasing profit:

■ Every business will own some form of IP.
■ The importance of IP is increasing.

- An effective IP strategy can protect market position.
- An effective IP strategy can give competitive advantage.
- An effective IP strategy may provide the incentive investors are looking for.

Be it a patentable invention, a new brand identity, a new design or a copy-right work (words, pictures, film, music, software), then obtaining and enforcing IP rights is often the only way to ensure that your creativity is not exploited by someone else.

TRADE MARKS

Do place value on your trade mark; it can often be the single most valuable marketing tool you own, whatever the size of business. A registered trade mark (RTM) can provide protection for the goodwill and reputation of a firm in its products and services. The owner of an RTM has the right to stop someone using the same or similar mark on the same or similar goods and services.

Don't forget that provided sufficient trading reputation and goodwill have been built up in a mark, a degree of protection is afforded by common law. However, in order to succeed in an action based on an unregistered mark, it is necessary to show both that one has established a reputation in the mark and that the use complained of would be liable to confuse or deceive the public.

Remember to check that the name of your product or company is original. It can be a severe psychological and financial blow to create a 'new' brand and start using this brand on a range of products, stationery, shop signs, etc, only to find that you are infringing an existing registered trade mark. A good starting point would be to check the trade mark register at www.patent. gov.uk.

Remember that RTMs are territorial; a UK RTM will offer protection only within these shores. There are simplified procedures for registration for the whole of the EU and internationally.

PATENTS

Do consider patent protection for novel products and processes. You do not have to apply for a patent to protect your product or processes – you could rely on keeping the information confidential. But without a patent you would lack the right to stop others from making, selling or importing the product or process you have developed.

Don't be blinded by your own good idea – check what else is out there; a scan of the published literature to establish what is already known can save you a lot of time and money. A good starting point is the patent database accessible from www.patent.gov.uk.

Remember that patents can be very expensive; you are in business to make money, so will a patent be worth obtaining? Will it be worth protecting in foreign markets?

Remember that patents are territorial; a UK patent will offer protection only within these shores. There are simplified procedures for patent protection across Europe and internationally.

DESIGNS

Do think about appearance; the outward shape or configuration of products of all kinds is protectable by either a registered design or a design right.

Don't overlook the fact that appearance may be crucial for the market success or failure of the product, whatever its other attributes. So a new mechanism in a camera will be patentable, but the 'look' of the casing that encloses the mechanism will be protectable by a registered design or the design right. The design can be of the product itself (or part of the product) or its pattern.

Remember that registered designs are territorial; a UK registered design will offer protection only within these shores. A single application to OHIM (oami.eu.int) gives protection for the whole of the EU.

COPYRIGHT

Do appreciate the value of any original literary, dramatic, musical and artistic works you may create. This will include your brochures, your website, software etc. They will be automatically protected by copyright. This right enables the creators to control exploitation and covers copying, adapting, publishing, performing and broadcasting.

Don't forget that generally the owner of copyright is the first creator or author, or their employer if produced in the ordinary course of their employment. But beware when using a contractor! A contractor will retain copyright ownership in the work unless their contract is explicit to the contrary.

Remember that there is no registration system for copyright in this country; it comes into existence automatically.

DOES THIS REALLY APPLY TO MY COMPANY?

IP is not the exclusive domain of large corporations. Smaller businesses, if well informed, can gain a great deal. Conversely, failure to recognize IP can prove costly.

Recent surveys suggest that the level of awareness of IP in the UK is very low. Many SMEs are largely unaware of their IP assets, and the majority do not have a system in place to carry out any form of IP audit to identify these assets. Indeed, most SMEs do not believe they have any IP!

However, businesses that adopt procedures to identify their IP assets can benefit in a number of ways:

- Generate income from licensing their IP.
- Increase the value of the business.
- Avoid potential wasteful investment in Research and Development.
- Protect identity through trade marks and branding.
- Open new markets.

Could your business benefit from finding out about IP?

For more information on Intellectual Property visit or contact The Patent Office Central Enquiry Unit by telephone on 08459 500 505 (charged at local rate) or e-mail enquiries@patent.gov.uk.

1.8

Raising funds

*Ian Ritchie, one of Scotland's leading business angels,
discusses how best to secure funds to turn bright
ideas into real companies*

OK, you have a bright idea, and it just, just, might turn out to have commercial potential. In fact, it might even form the basis of a new business – so what do you actually do next?

You know a great deal about your area of technology, who the main researchers are and what stage they are at, and you know that none of them can quite achieve what you can do. You have a couple of colleagues who can be persuaded to join you in your new adventure (but do try to ensure that at least one of your team has some commercial experience). You even believe that it is quite possible that you might be able to get a product or service into the market significantly ahead of any competition.

But what you don't know is: how exactly do you go about building and financing a business?

How do you actually go about: renting an office; getting a company registered; getting the logo, the stationery, and the website done? How do you employ staff – do they need contracts? How do you find and appoint accountants and lawyers? How do you go about raising the funding? How do you get your company noticed – all the things that make your bright idea into a real company?

Well, the first thing to do is to network. You will, of course, know your way around the technology community of which you are a part. Now you must inject yourself into a new community – among people of a more entrepreneurial bent. You need to put yourself about where people who have run successful technology businesses hang out. Find the local entrepreneurs' club; there will probably be one near you. The massive enthusiasm that drove the First Tuesday movement in the late nineties may have dispelled, but many of the gatherings started then still take place under another name.

The key person that you are looking for is known as a 'business angel'. This will be an individual who has built a business and sold it, and who is looking potentially to get involved in another start-up company. Ideally a business angel will have experience in an area related to yours, and be willing to contribute both money and time to your project, be willing to join your board and advise you on all the various intricacies of building a business from scratch.

You may even find one or more groups of business angels in your area – they tend to hunt in packs! If so, you should cultivate a relationship with them and try to find the one who has the right kind of experience for you.

Contact your Regional Enterprise Agency. They will have people whose job it is to help businesses like yours get started. Make sure that you get advice from a senior experienced executive, though, don't just take what they hand out at their 'business shop' to potential hairdressers and window cleaners.

Find a good accountant. Again, ask around. Find out which firms have helped other new businesses to get started, and who have given appropriate advice on the early stages of a company – a time when the financial affairs of your business may not be substantial, but when it is vitally important to get it right. Fees are important here. The right accountant will be the one that understands that the fees he or she can charge you at the outset must be low, on the understanding that there should be years of profitable relationship ahead in the future.

You will need to write a business plan. This can be a bit unnerving at first and more often than not leads to the creation of some of the worst documents that have ever been written. Somehow or other, otherwise inspiring and creative people seem to freeze up and become slow and lumbering when required to write a business plan.

But it is really not so difficult. Remember that a business plan is basically a selling document – it has to act as your salesperson with your potential investors. First of all, it needs to inspire and excite, give a clear picture of what it is that you offer, why it is that you can create it ahead of any potential competition, and how you are going to sell it.

And keep it short, really short. Around a dozen pages are usually quite enough. Remember that people in the investment community get several business plans every day, many of which run to over a hundred pages of closely-spaced grey type. Just put yourself in their place and consider the effect of a 10-page plan arriving on their desk. For a start, they will probably read it first.

Your business plan should concentrate on the commercialization of your idea or technology. The technical detail should not be explained in any great detail in the plan itself, but the commercial application of it should be. If your technology is the key to your project it may be appropriate to attach an Appendix to the plan with the necessary technical detail.

Concentrate on the commercial opportunity. Explain how you will sell your product or service, identifying the likely channels to market. Introduce your team – investors like to invest in an impressive team and you should make sure that you play up the strengths of your colleagues.

You should include three years of financial forecasts – one page each for the profit and loss, balance sheet and cash flow – but don't make too much of a meal of the financials. It is much more important that you, as the principal of the project, thoroughly understand and can explain the financial projections, rather than having huge quantities of financial figures that you barely understand prepared for you by an accountant.

Consider attending one or more investment forums. These are events at which new or growing businesses have 10 or 15 minutes to pitch their business ideas to an audience of potential investors, usually followed by break-out sessions at which more detailed discussions can be held. It is quite probable that at an investment forum you will meet people who are particularly interested in investing in your type of project.

Then pick on a few investment companies to whom to pitch your idea. You can find details of potential investment companies via the website of the British Venture Capital Association (www.bvca.co.uk). You should read the details of each investment company carefully and target your proposal to the ones that are most likely to make the kind of investment you need (amounts of money invested, stage of investment undertaken, technology sector etc).

It is best, if at all possible, to get an introduction to the companies that you target via someone that knows them. It is always better to have a warm introduction; it reduces the possibility that your plan will end up, essentially unread, in the dustbin. Ask around; your business angel should be of some help here, as should your accountants and lawyers. If you really don't have any success with this it may be worth while hiring a specialist advisory company to help you raise your money. However, you should remember that investors are often suspicious of such intermediaries and if they are really interested will want to deal with you directly.

Then, it is just a matter of negotiating the deal. Here, it is of considerable advantage to have someone on your side (such as your business angel) that has some experience of this process. What you want is the simplest possible deal, with the investors paying cash for ordinary shares. What they often ask for is a variety of preference shares or loan stock, where they have more financial protection if the business does not ultimately end up reaching its potential.

As with all such deals, the more investors that you have chasing you, the better. Competition is by far the best way to keep the investors honest, and to get the best deal. But bear in mind that you want investors who can follow their money in future, and who are unlikely to panic if you have future problems in implementing your plans. So pick investors with lots of relevant experience.

So that's it really. In summary you should:

- Get a good team around you, keeping in mind that you should, if possible, have somebody on your team with a commercial background.
- Find a good business angel with relevant experience.
- Appoint a good accountant who is used to dealing with start-up businesses.
- Write a punchy, highly attractive, business plan. Keep it short. Remember it is a selling document.
- Create a compelling presentation, and sign up for an investment forum at which to pitch it.
- Select a few relevant investment companies (from the BVCA website) and get somebody to introduce you to them if you can.

Then all you have to do is to negotiate the best deal that you can.

More information: www.coppertop.co.uk.

Part 2

Creative behaviour

Creative culture

*Creativity is a behaviour, not a process, argues brand-expert
Jane Asscher, managing director of 23red*

Innovation has never before held such a high value. The share price of 'high innovation intensity' companies in the FTSE 100 has outperformed the FTSE 100 index every year for the last six years (source: Department of Trade and Industry: R&D score board 2003).

While technical brilliance, original insights and efficient processes are key to this, it is creative marketing ideas that separate the 5 per cent of new products that succeed from the 95 per cent that fail.

BAN THE WORD 'INNOVATION' IN CREATIVE ENVIRONMENTS

I'd be in *The Sunday Times* Rich List if I had a penny for every marketing creative brief that asked for a 'big, innovative idea'. If only it were so easy. Such briefs assume that creativity, rather like innovation, is a process. They also assume that creativity is the preserve of those with 'creative' in their title. It is neither. Creativity is a behaviour. Creative ideas are the product of motivated, talented, integrated groups of people sparking off each other and their environment. The catalyst is the inspirational culture of the organization to which they belong.

Having grappled with this on many occasions, in creative businesses from large corporate groups to small enterprises, I have come to realize there is no one-size-fits-all solution to defining and propagating an inspirational culture, but there are a number of areas to consider.

This chapter seeks to provide helpful ideas on how to foster a culture of inspiration, make it part of everyday life and create an organization that inspires creative behaviour.

INSPIRATIONAL VISION AND VALUES

Clearly defining a vision and values for an organization is key to defining its culture. An inspirational vision is an essential prerequisite to promoting a creative culture. Orange, for example, launched in April 1994 into the UK mobile communications market with a simple vision: a brighter future, where people can communicate wherever, whenever and however they wish. Today that commitment remains the same, as does the commitment to the values of service, choice, quality and innovation. This commitment, which interestingly does not reference mobile phones, has ensured that Orange is consistently lauded for customer service and regularly first to market with new innovations.

Of course, culturally defining vision and values can be communicated internally via job descriptions, staff handbooks etc. But defining the creative culture of an organization is only the start. It must be nurtured, championed and propagated tirelessly. Consideration needs to be given to organizational structure, people strategies and management practices, the role of external influences, the working environment and practical tools to develop and support ideas.

INTEGRATED ORGANIZATIONAL STRUCTURE

Encouragement for creative approaches must come from the top. Break down departmental silos and create opportunities for teams to focus and organize around the 'customer', wherever possible. Relationships must be characterized by honesty and openness and the organization needs to show itself to be flexible and open to change.

MOTIVATING PEOPLE

Recruiting people on the basis of their ability to inspire ideas and to work as part of a team is a good place to start, so try to embed this into every job description. Encourage people to work together to develop their creative potential by allocating part of your training budget to creative skills. This will give them the confidence to be creative, but it is recognition and reward that will reap long-term benefits. This means identifying management practices that foster teamwork and inspire ideas – and expressing appreciation of staff that exhibit them. Such practices might include 'building open and trusting relationships', 'participation in problem solving via team working', 'commitment to change and individual autonomy' and 'an obsessive commitment to customers and staff'. Logically, this means evaluating employees' performance against these criteria, and acknowledging this via a performance-related component to remuneration. Importantly, the objective-setting and appraisal process must drive continual improvement and recognize that failure is part of the learning experience.

On the softer side, instigating a benefits package that promotes work–life balance will engender staff loyalty. Promoting the benefits of time out and giving staff a creative allowance to spend on cultural activities help to open minds, and plenty of team social get-togethers help bonding. Designing creative ways to get their feedback can further stimulate their creativity.

HARNESSING EXTERNAL INFLUENCES

Involving people from outside the team or organization can generate new perspectives. Consider running workshops with stakeholders – suppliers, strategic partners and customers. External moderators or facilitators can often help bring objectivity to the exercise. Encourage staff to attend networking events, conferences and lectures. Invite key opinion formers, influencers, academics and trend spotters to come in and share their thinking.

MAXIMIZING THE ENVIRONMENT

Create an environment where employees feel part of a team and where they have the space and stimulus to spark, but remember to include mini-environments that embrace different needs. The most creative environments promote flexibility and workspace mobility. Open-plan areas encourage spontaneous idea sharing and dedicated project spaces allow for focused collaboration. Comfortably furnished spaces plastered with stimulus material spark brainstorms. Quiet spaces are essential for allowing people to contemplate, capture and craft creative ideas. Giving communal spaces a function promotes interaction at every opportunity. For example, a reception area can become a social hub (coffee shop by day/bar and games room by night).

PRACTICAL TECHNIQUES TO SUPPORT AND DEVELOP IDEAS

Faced with a barrage of information, it can be difficult for your team to see the wood for the trees. Practical insight generation tools such as market and mind maps can often help to identify that single insight, framing a focused proposition to which you can apply creative skills. They don't give you the answer, but they do provide a structure for organizing and analysing information. Similarly, idea generation or brainstorms can help to break up rigidly established patterns, reinterpret the problem and promote lateral thinking.

BE FREE, IN A STRUCTURED WAY

Of course, the key to creativity is freedom. The trick is harnessing that freedom to best effect for your business. Use guidelines: facilitate, set goals and time limits, encourage fun, separate idea generation from evaluation, include a mix of personalities and, above all, remember that no idea is a bad idea. With a creative conscience across your business structure, you'll find that a creative culture can permeate throughout.

Jane Asscher is managing partner and chairman of 23red, an agency created to focus on brand-centric ideas, leveraging them across all media. She advises clients, including the UK government, Flextech and the World Rally Championship, on integrated marketing.

2.2

Creative skills

In 37 years at Unilever, Richard Duggan survived 50 failed attempts to launch products and processes into international markets. However, he gained enough experience, and the kudos from 50 more successful launches to become senior industrial innovation advisor to the Innovation Group, DTI for nine years. He now helps individuals and companies release their latent creativity and radically improve their innovation performance

The failure until recently of UK Business Schools to teach Innovation as a practical topic has had a strongly adverse effect on the wealth of the nation. Apart from working in innovative companies, there has been no platform of best practice experience on which young would-be innovators could stand. This neglect partly provides the answer to the question often posed by the media: *Why is Britain so good at discovering the fundamental principles on which sunrise industries are based (creativity) and so poor in translating them into wealth for the nation (innovation)?*

WHERE DOES CREATIVITY END AND INNOVATION BEGIN?

Creativity – thinking of novel and appropriate ideas. Innovation – the successful implementation of those ideas within an organization. (Dr W Coyne, 3M, The UK Innovation Lecture 1996)

This definition of the relationship of **creativity** and **innovation**, delivered from the perspective of the most consistently innovative company over more than 50 years, captures very well the relationship of these two words. Creativity is a concept in your head. Innovation is a process covering every aspect of the complex series of events required to turn the idea into a successful reality. It is a chain in which the improbability of a successful outcome depends on whether the weakest link in the whole business mix is at least strong enough. The lack of understanding of this issue is a major reason why such a high proportion of externally focused attempts at innovation fail – and why, though Britain is a nation of inventors, so few of the inventions lead to profitable outcomes.

THE ANATOMY OF INNOVATION

A helpful insight on innovation resulted from the 1998 EIRMAYIX study on 'Creativity and Innovativeness within R&D'. EIRMA, the European Industrial Research Managers Association, has as members over 160 of the leading companies of Europe which invest significantly in R&D. Thirty-two participated in the study, and many more validated the outcome. The conclusions portrayed innovation as a four-stage process:

- Creativity – the source of the novel idea.
- Culture – is the instant internal reaction to a radical idea to seek value or to look for reasons to reject or debunk it?
- Cross-functional teamworking – do members of teams set up to translate the idea into a feasible option, have a 'can do' attitude and go 'the extra mile' for each other, or simply defend departmental territory?
- An effective innovation process. Is there a systematic process to check at each stage whether all the issues which must be considered in the right sequence have been resolved?

Considering this model, how are modern organizations responding to the challenge of being innovative?

Many broadly attempt to develop climates in which staff are encouraged to submit ideas, they train teams to develop some internal momentum and many have an innovation process in place. Most, though, neglect two major aspects of this holistic approach to innovation.

They do not complement their procedural system for innovation review (most usually StageGate (trade mark of R.G. Cooper)) with a conceptual process. The systematic checklist is not backed by a good theoretical understanding of the leading-edge principles of each functional skill as it becomes important during the process from idea to market. For example, Prof Cooper in StageGate points out that 50 per cent of all failed attempts at innovation result from insufficient attention to understanding the market for the product. Would-be innovators instead focus on product research. If the product is good they do not consider whether the market is a good or poor one to enter. Surprisingly few are aware of Michael Porter's work defining the characteristics that define a good market to select for entry:

If you want to be rich, go where the money is. (President J F Kennedy)

The second and chronic area of neglect is that companies make only very amateur attempts to harness the latent creativity of their workforce.

BREAKOUT CREATIVITY

If an idea is not at first absurd there is no hope for it. (att. Albert Einstein)

When teaching groups or individuals how to access their latent creativity, we show them how the barriers that formal education inadvertently builds inhibit their ability to see issues in new perspectives. The work of Jack Foster in his entertaining book *How to Get Ideas* is a good start. His brilliant marketing students individually found it harder to respond to the challenge, 'Develop a novel campaign for Coca-Cola over lunchtime', than 'Develop 100 novel campaigns for Coca-Cola over lunchtime':

'Why is it more difficult to produce one idea than one hundred ideas?'
'Well, one idea has to be your best, whereas with one hundred you don't have time to evaluate.'
'But Osbourne's first principle of creativity is never evaluate while creating. Do you mean you are evaluating ideas while still thinking of them? What criteria are you using?'
'Whether they are good ideas – practical.'

> *'But if an idea is at first absurd, there is no hope for it. Are you therefore rejecting all the potential breakout ideas in favour of the marginal but practical proposals?'*

This captures the central issue of why so little of the latent creative potential of individuals and whole workforces is deployed to solve business problems and drive innovation. As young children we are all spectacularly creative.

'LOOKING WHERE EVERYONE ELSE IS LOOKING AND SEEING WHAT NO ONE ELSE CAN SEE' ALBERT SZENT-GYORGI

Early encounters with formal education rapidly teach us to be critical and evaluative – to see what everyone else agrees is sensible and practical. Our divergent creativity gets submerged deep in our subconscious minds. However, the creativity is still latent. It is rather easily accessed with a little training to short-circuit the barriers of immediate practicality which our own minds build as mental defences against looking foolish or practically unsound.

Use of creativity courses

The way we approach creative training is to invite participants to bring to a mentoring programme two real problems which they are very keen to solve and to implement the new solutions. They are carefully briefed in advance on what constitutes a really challenging creative problem. Groups, ideally of eight, are then videoed attempting to solve the problems. Immediately afterwards they analyse the tapes, answering 'What ideas and behaviours helped to solve the problem?' 'What needs improving?' Over three days they discover for themselves the self-destructive barriers to allowing really new ideas to flourish. They learn how to overcome them; the importance of not leaping straight from idea to solution, or evaluating in the normal binary good idea/bad idea mode. They start seeing strange ideas as valuable stepping stones to ideal problem solutions. In their baseline session, before mentoring, we normally expect a group to produce perhaps five ideas which the problem owner considers novel. After the 16 sessions of a typical course for 16 people, in a session of similar duration to the baseline, a typical outcome would be over 100 novel ideas with 5–8 worked up into potential solutions. Once learnt, with some practice, these new-found creative competences become life skills.

Creative processes to overcome mental resistance to breakout thinking

The mentoring process described captures many of the features of Synectics, which is one of the 114 creative processes which Michael Hicks identified in his 1993 study of the literature on creativity.

These processes are all designed to unlock creative potential by tackling one or other of the mental barriers to creativity built up by society. Over 50 of them, based often on different underlying principles, are called 'Brainstorming'. Despite this, even notionally innovative organizations, such as leading R&D establishments vitally interested in problem solving, usually rely on some generic 'brainstorming' technique as their problem-solving process. They have no awareness that such processes are horses for courses, and an inappropriate process selected for a particular problem is unlikely to be effective.

We usually use Synectics as one of our core training processes because it has evolved over 40 years from intensive scrutiny of the behaviour of individuals in creative groups, into a family of coherent sub-processes. These tackle creativity at every stage, from generating breakout ideas, through selecting ideas on grounds of novelty and intrigue for further development, to the process of turning speculative concepts into highly practical solutions.

Most other processes concentrate purely on developing novel ideas, and, unlike Synectics, do not have a constant process of behavioural refinement to hone them into highly effective working tools. Nevertheless, they can be highly effective in specific circumstances and in training courses we seek to provide a grounding in a wide range of such approaches. Here, Hicks' work again is useful. He identifies that the myriad of identified techniques are derived from three core approaches: Osborne Parnes Brainstorming, Synectics and Morphological Analysis.

This latter technique, a favourite of my early attempts at innovation, is far more systematic than its peers. Using a spreadsheet, it attempts to show novel solutions to a problem by studying successful solutions in some distant parallel environment. While much neglected nowadays, it is very powerful in, for example, identifying for patent protection fields for an invention very different from those for which it was originally envisaged.

THE OUTCOME OF MENTORING

Our experience from helping organizations unlock creative potential is that about half of all attendees embrace the approaches in their regular business life, with a significant number taking on the challenge of developing sufficient experience to be trained as internal mentors for their organization. However, there is an annoying tendency for people to think creativity is like a best suit – only for special occasions – when breakout ideas are needed to solve problems or drive the business forward. Yet creativity is required in all stages of the innovation process, and we have recently started work with clients mentoring them on fast tracking the later stages of innovation without waiting to assemble the highly resourced teams which conventional business practice premise as necessary. The stage of moving from an approved idea to a quantified draft business plan is usually allocated resource over, say, a four-week period, usually with heavy overrun. By reconfiguring the sub-processes as creative challenges posing creative questions, 'what expert in any field would instantly know the answer to this aspect of the issue?', we like to demonstrate that the bulk of this stage can be handled by a competent group with access to modern information in one day, sometimes in one hour! Shades of my Unilever experience, when our attempts at improving the speed of changeover from filling detergent in one pack size to another, by benchmarking across the Unilever companies worldwide, produced gradual improvements. With a new insight, perhaps 10 minutes could be pared off 16 hours. When we targeted, instead, the Williams Formula One team, who change tyres and refill petrol in under 10 seconds, results improved spectacularly!

RELEASING THE CREATIVITY OF WHOLE WORKFORCES

The Partnership with People study was set up by the Innovation Unit DTI to study how companies learn to harness the talent of whole organizations. I was involved in the fieldwork and I and my board at Crosfield Chemicals decided to use the learning to create an innovation culture in the company – a 175-year-old Merseyside-based business with a long-standing command and control culture. Guided by consultants from Quest Worldwide each board member and a shop floor colleague, as two-person teams, were trained to teach empowerment to all our 650 UK employees. The essence of the training was that rather than 'the job description' governing an individual's daily actions, everyone has the responsibility and authority to use their skills to the full to further the company's goals and aspirations. A new emphasis on ideas from all was backed by a system in which every idea submitted had a first response within three days, and the norm was 'good idea – do it'! Whenever possible, the idea owner leads the implementation – regardless of status, because that person has the best understanding of the concept and the highest motivation to achieve a successful outcome.

This initiative, with the backing of a committed board, had an instant payback in the first year, with 1,000 ideas implemented. The total profit deriving from ideas was of the order of the previous trading profit, and we also achieved a radical change in the internal culture.

In parallel, partners in my current business, Vincent Nolan, and Martin Brooks of Changemaker, represented one arm of the several groups brought into Asda by Leighton and Norman in the early 1990s to achieve radical change across all aspects of Asda's, then, failing performance. The processes invented for achieving a low-bureaucracy, customer-focused, 'can do' culture are described in the book and CD by Nolan and Martin *The Changemaker's Toolkit*. The emergence of Asda within the decade as the winner of the *Sunday Times* 'Best company to work for' helps debunk the myth that one can only change internal culture very slowly. Culture can be modified rather quickly by behavioural training if there is a totally congruent business message supported by the behaviour and body language of the whole management team.

ADVICE TO COMPANIES SEEKING TO INCREASE THEIR INNOVATIVE PERFORMANCE

Innovation requires a culture of constant improvement, backed by occasional 'frighten the competition' breakthrough. To achieve the latter 'externally focused' innovation requires great business attention and competence in all functions, and it is difficult for senior management to manage simultaneously a process of constant internal improvement and breakout innovation. Hence the internal innovation must become systemic – needing little top-management attention, and if this requires a culture change, it is essential to train everyone in the new behaviours required. Issuing booklets, announcing open door policies, changing structures and procedures does not work. **Changing behaviour is only achieved by people experiencing the new behaviours. All internal processes, such as appraisal, informal reward systems, informal criteria of respect winning and the body language of the whole management team, must also be aligned to support the new culture.** Changing the physical environment can be a powerful indicator of the 'new regime', and all such moves should be considered from the perspective of how they can help optimize the best aspect of the required culture and reinforce the new required aspects.

Teaching creative skill is a very practical way of encouraging more innovative behaviour. The creativity taught can be harnessed to invent the processes needed to achieve the new dimensions of innovation required, and the creative team building and 'can do' problem solving greatly aid the drive to turn embryo inventions into profit.

SELF-EXAMINATION FOR A HOLISTIC INNOVATION STRATEGY

Have you an innovative internal culture with everyone striving for continual improvement? If there is a good flow of suggestions, do you seek to enhance the quality by teaching staff how to harness their innate creativity? Is the culture receptive to challenging ideas, and are the criteria of acceptance novelty and interest, or immediate practicality? Are cross-functional teams dynamic and creative?

Have you a well-understood innovation process at both the procedural and conceptual level? Do the leaders of innovations understand the huge difference between the skills and role of an innovation process manager and those who lead conventional project management?

At last, a number of business schools such as Cranfield and Strathclyde are looking at the practical aspects of innovation delivery and there are mentoring organizations such as the Synectics Company, What if? or the network of experts on innovation, change management and creativity which my own company Duggan Creative represents, to help with the process of utilizing to the full the total skills of the whole organization.

'Buy a pair of hands and the brain comes as a free optional extra!'

Richard is CEO of Duggan Creative, Innovation Advisors. He has been involved for over 30 years in harnessing the latent creativity of individuals and groups, and turning ideas into innovation. This work has resulted in launch of over 100 products and processes into global markets, and appearance as an Innovation awards finalist on Tomorrow's World.

Richard was the Senior Industrial Innovation Advisor to the Innovation Unit of the UK Department of Trade and Industry from 1993–2002, having previously been a founder member of the UK Government Advisory Committee on Innovation. Richard graduated from Liverpool University with a first-class Honours degree in Organic Chemistry. His industrial background was 37 years in Unilever in a wide variety of roles always associated with innovation. He is a visiting professor at John Moores University and has had many roles associated with effective teaching of Science and Technology.

His company, Duggan Creative, is a skills mentoring organization focused on releasing the reservoir of latent creativity in individuals and whole workforces, and developing effective innovation processes to turn such ideas rapidly into profitable outcomes. Skills include creating an innovation culture, facilitation and facilitation mentoring, building creative teams and implementing conceptual and procedural innovation processes. The client base ranges from 'blue chip' companies across Europe and America to public sector organizations, networks and fast-growth small companies.

2.3

Products to fit customers

Build close relationships with customers and create designs around their needs, advises 3M's Pip Frankish. That way you can revolutionize markets

Talk about 'innovation', and what customers want, and consumer goods immediately spring to mind. We think of a Dyson vacuum cleaner that sucks dust better than its rivals or the latest Nokia mobile phone which does just about everything – except vacuuming.

But understanding customer needs is equally important where there is no glossy consumer finished product. What about components or equipment for industrial markets? – competition, driving the need for differentiation, is equally fierce.

Giving customers what they want means understanding the market and, more importantly, the concerns of the customer. What keeps them awake at night? What do they want to change – and, importantly, why?

To understand these concepts, we will look at the car repair industry. If you have had the misfortune to damage your car, you may have first-hand experience. You know what you want – the dent removed and the car repaired so no one can ever tell it happened. But what about the person running the car repair workshop? He is a customer too – he has to buy equipment and consumables to run his operation. And, as in other industries, he is continually challenged by external factors.

The ownership and structure of the car repair business is undergoing unprecedented change. The size of the business – estimated to be worth €51 billion in 2005 in Northern Europe alone (Germany, France, Italy, Spain, the Netherlands, Belgium and the UK) – means that major companies, or holding operations, are entering the market and amalgamating smaller repair shops into groups. Until 10 years ago, most car repair shops in Europe were owned and run as small family businesses. It is estimated that today there are 100,000 car body shops across Europe, with as many as 65 per cent of these now owned by a corporate organization looking to run an industrial operation rather than a small commercial business.

The car repair industry's challenges represent opportunities for innovation. 3M is a company close to the car industry; its connection with the automotive industry goes right back to its roots. Many of the company's first customers were in the automotive manufacturing industry and it now supplies a range of products to car manufacturers – from structural adhesives which are used to bond body parts instead of traditional welding, to solar-reflecting glazing film. In addition, 3M also has a thriving Automotive Aftercare Division, serving the car repair industry.

3M's closeness to the car repair industry provides a strong network. Over the years, it has built relationships by investing time in direct sales calls to the car repair shops – even though these end-users buy repair consumable products from distributors. The company's reputation for delivering solutions is renowned and its diverse technology capability means it has developed a unique intimacy with end-users which is unmatched as market leader.

The 3M sales team calling on the car repair shops understands the processes involved in car repairs. The team is driven by a determination to match customer needs with cost-effective solutions to improve the customers' business – rather than merely using incentives and promotions to sell commodity products. Each team member aims to understand the industry and how repair shops are having to change to stay ahead in the fiercely competitive market.

Such detailed understanding has led to innovations such as 3M's Soft Edge Masking Foam Tape and 3M™ Trizact™ Fine Finishing abrasive discs. In both these cases the need was not articulated by the end-user but was identified by the 3M team through observation and conversation around specific issues encountered when re-spraying car panels.

In addition to observation in repair shops and the ongoing dialogue between the sales teams and end-users, regular focus groups and panel discussions are held. Towards the end of the 1990s these were focused on the financial and environmental challenges facing body repair shops.

The discussions revealed that the car repair business was becoming more competitive. And not just because of the shift in ownership. Cars may be cheaper to buy but they are becoming more expensive to repair because of more sophisticated designs. As insurance costs soar, the insurance industry, which funds most car repairs, is struggling to keep premiums down and make a profit. It is demanding better-quality repairs at cheaper prices from the repair shops.

In addition, legislation is impacting the industry. Emissions legislation, which initially concentrated on the manufacturing industry, is now focused on smaller industries; by 2007 all car repair shops in Europe have to reduce volatile organic compound (VOC) emissions. Safety legislation is also increasing.

These financial and environmental concerns present ongoing pressures for those running car repair workshops. During discussions a number of specific needs were articulated. But 3M also identified some unarticulated needs – things customers wanted though they couldn't describe them.

The 3M team set about the process of developing ideas and solutions. Over three years a focused development team worked on the project. One particular need they had identified was improving the paint-spraying process. This involved mixing paint to achieve the colour match, filtering to ensure it was dust free, before pouring it into a pot, then attaching the pot to a spray-gun which could only be used in a vertical position. Following the application, excess paint was disposed of and the pot and gun had to be washed in solvents in a machine which, typically, was leased. The process was messy, laborious, costly and resulted in VOC emissions from the solvents used.

Previous manufacturers had attempted to develop modifications to existing products to improve the process and had failed. 3M set about looking at the problem from a different angle by using 'white space' thinking – asking 'what does the customer need to solve these problems?'

The result was 3M™ Paint Preparation System (PPS) – a unique closed paint system that eliminates the need for separate mixing cups and filters. Instead, paint is mixed in a 'liner bag', which marries to a direct filter lid and is then mounted on a spray-gun using a special adapter. As freshly filtered paint is dispensed, the liner bag collapses, allowing the spray-gun to function at any angle. Disposable parts – ie the liner bag and filter lid – are made from similar materials to allow for recycling, leaving only the spray-gun to be cleaned. Excess paint can remain in the liner bags and be capped and stored for later use. This means a more efficient use of paint, a 70 per cent reduction in solvents, reduced VOCs and an improved working environment.

Over the three years there were numerous iterations to achieve this. Significant design hurdles were overcome by inverting the spray-gun before connection. This also gave the product total differentiation from anything else on the market.

PPS was launched in the UK in July 2000 and was successful immediately. It offered an ingenious solution that not only helped the customer do his job better but also helped make his business more successful. Changes to long-standing working practices are rarely acceptable to industrial customers unless demonstrable process and financial benefits can be seen. And customer satisfaction is of paramount importance in any market to initiate and sustain sales.

PPS has since been rolled out across mainland Europe and is now being rolled out internationally. It is covered by numerous patents and has achieved an innovation award from the UK Design Council and numerous trade awards for innovation, including Body Shop Product of the Year for Europe in 2001.

Innovation is about more than an idea. To develop a commercially successful product in a commodity market requires an ability to listen to customers and an understanding of market pressures to ensure the exact nature of the business opportunity. In this way the product design meets the customer need – and it's a sure way to a product that sells.

Pip Frankish is General Manager, Corporate Marketing & Communication at 3M UK plc, where she leads a team of in-house consultants, providing specialist communications and strategic marketing expertise to 3M business units. 3M is an $18 billion diversified technology company providing innovative solutions to customers in health care, safety, electronics, telecommunications, industrial, consumer and office supplies, and other markets.

2.4

Inspirational leadership

If you want really effective innovation,
only inspirational leadership will do,
says Nigel Crouch in the DTI's Innovation Group

Only those companies who are able to innovate effectively throughout the organization will survive and prosper in the ever more demanding and fast-changing world in which we all now have to operate. And really effective innovation will only happen if the leaders of those companies inspire it through their people – all their people.

Everybody in the organization has got to want to contribute to the process. Over and above the more obvious areas like the research and development laboratories and the marketing department, people need to be fully involved in continually coming up with better ways of doing things to improve the operation and keep ahead of the competition everywhere in the organization. This includes the finance department, personnel administration and, perhaps most crucially, the shop floor and the customer-facing sharp-end of the business.

SO HOW ARE WE DOING ON INSPIRING OUR PEOPLE?

In a major survey of over 1,500 managers conducted by the Chartered Management Institute and Demos, people were asked what they would most like to see in their leaders. The single most important factor by a very significant margin, which was highlighted by 55 per cent of the sample, was 'Inspiration' but only 11 per cent actually saw this 'Ability to Inspire' in their leaders. The top two attributes actually observed were 'Knowledge' and 'Ambition'!

The very latest research from the Institute paints an even more alarming picture. Seventy-nine per cent of respondents want to see a genuinely shared vision in their organization but only 38 per cent actually see one. There are similar gaps on what people desire from their leaders in terms of trust and respect, and 62 per cent of those questioned felt that their leaders were out of touch with what their people are feeling. Perhaps most depressing was the fact that one-third of followers admit that they have never, throughout their careers, worked for an inspirational leader.

TRADITIONAL LEADERSHIP INNOVATION BLOCKERS

Your archetypal traditional leader is the biggest single blocker of effective innovation. One of the great drivers of innovation is ignorance. Some of the best innovations happen because people ask naïve, uninformed questions. How many traditional leaders do you know who are willing to admit to ignorance?

Another key driver for innovation is diversity, with people coming at issues from very different perspectives feeling totally free to express their different points of view. Innovation thrives on positive dissent. How many traditional leaders do you know who are comfortable with any form of dissent, which they see as undermining their authority?

Leading effective innovation is all about revelling in the success of other people. To foster innovation, leaders have to want other people to be more successful than they are and – even more challenging – be prepared to take the blame for other people's failures! How many traditional leaders do you know who are happy not to take personal credit for every success and pick up the blame for others' failures?

Innovation is also, and importantly, a very social activity within the workplace, requiring high levels of trust and collaboration. How many traditional leaders do you know who still tend to cut themselves off from their people, which is clearly not the ideal basis for mutual trust and genuine collaboration?

POINTERS TO INSPIRATIONAL LEADERSHIP

So how do we move away from the traditional leadership model and really start to close this critical leadership 'inspiration' gap to achieve optimum innovation?

Several ongoing DTI 'business sharing with business' leading-edge practice programmes being driven with a number of lead partners provide a number of powerful pointers as to what makes for inspirational leadership. These programmes include 'Living Innovation' and the '100 Best Companies to Work For', the latter produced by Best Companies (UK) and published annually by *The Sunday Times*.

Six essential elements of 'inspirational leadership' come through time and time again, despite the mix and broad spread of the different organizations involved.

Inspirational leaders genuinely care about their people

When you ask people what it's like to work in an organization run by an inspirational leader, they talk about openness, honesty, respect and trust. These are very friendly workplaces and people feel highly valued and regarded. When you walk around there is a sort of electricity in the air and you are struck by their incredible energy and buzz. And the leader puts it this way: 'There is no other source of competitive advantage. Others can copy our investment, technology and scale – but not the quality of our people!'

Inspirational leaders involve everybody

People are given considerable freedom – and support – to get on with the job and are highly motivated and fulfilled as a result. As another leader put it to us: 'We never use the word "empowerment". You can't empower people, you can only create the climate and structure in which they will take responsibility.'

Inspirational leaders listen a lot

They recognize that it is the people doing the job who generally know the solutions to the problems and they ask for and respect what their people tell them about how to do things better. As one of the respondents in the Partnerships with People programme put it: 'It is not the sole prerogative of the senior managers to come up with the good ideas.'

Inspirational leaders show lots of appreciation

Recognition is an absolutely crucial element of inspiration but we are not very good in the UK at saying 'thank you'. Yet those two words are a tremendous motivator when used genuinely at the right time.

And we came across some innovative ways in which inspirational leaders say 'thank you'. At the opticians Dolland and Aitchison, whom we visited in our Living Innovation programme, they have 'Incredible Colleague Awards'; staff who are successfully nominated can live out their 'incredible fantasies' courtesy of the company. Whether it is parachute jumping, driving a fast car round Silverstone or learning to dance the salsa, the company will make it happen for the 'great colleague' as a very special way of saying 'thank you'.

Inspirational leaders ensure work is fun

Fun is both a great indicator that an organization is innovative and a key driver for innovation. At the '100 Best Companies to Work For' you see a lot of fun at work, ranging from lots of celebration of success (something else we are not generally very good at in the UK!), to regular social nights out, to annual themed staff dinners. At the same time, they enjoy outstanding performance.

And finally, inspirational leaders and their people are deeply committed

They are passionate about creating something special for their customers and, no matter how well they are doing, they are always looking to do things better. They are the epitome of what James Dyson describes as 'the Restless Company'. And they are deeply committed to the attainment of the shared vision for the organization that they are all driving towards.

THE WAY FORWARD

An exciting new Leadership Programme is currently under way through the DTI and its Partners aimed at establishing an Inspirational Leadership Index, providing clear signposting to the best available Leadership Tools and mapping and helping to further develop Leadership Networks across the country. And it is worth the journey because inspirational leadership leads to inspirational results.

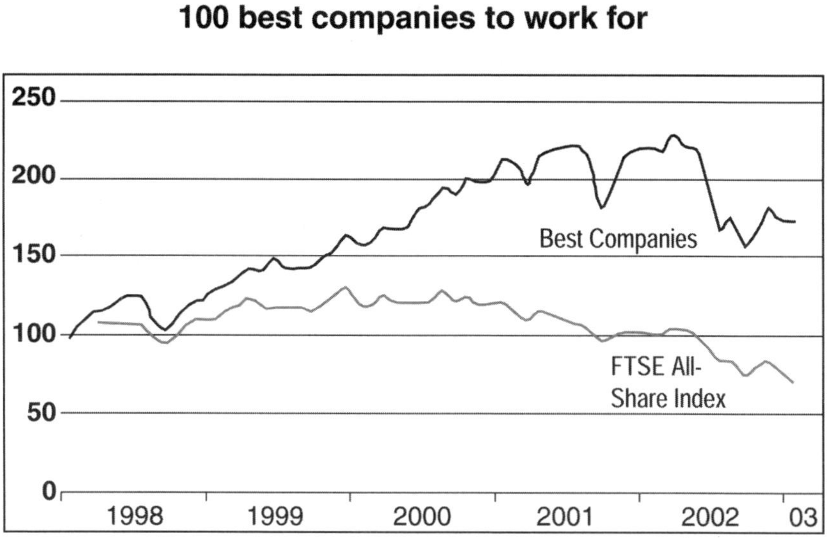

100 best companies to work for

Figure 2.4 *100 best companies to work for*

The final word on Inspirational Leadership goes to this middle manager in a highly innovative organization that we visited, who summed up how it feels like this:

'People are proud to work here. Proud of colleagues, proud of the company and proud of themselves.'

Copies of 'Achieving Best Practice in Your Business – Inspirational Leadership' (URN 04/1085) and '100 Best Companies to Work For' can be obtained on Order Line Telephone 0870 150 2500 or Fax 0870 150 2333. Also visit www.dti.gov.uk, www.innovation.gov.uk and www.Sunday-times.co.uk/bestcompanies.

Nigel Crouch is a Senior Industrialist who spends part of his time working with the DTI Innovation Group, where he is leading on the 'Inspirational Leadership' and '100 Best Companies to Work For' programmes.

2.5

Teaming and networking

Complex programme management requires many threads to operate in parallel, argues Garrick Jones of the Ludic Group.

Bringing new products and services to market requires the successful cooperation of many very different partners – including marketers, product and service designers, programme managers, IP lawyers, distributors, advertisers, supply chain managers, producers and packagers. In most cases these partners are working in parallel, kicking off processes which are vital to successful product launch long before the finished product has been completed. For example, Boeing created the 777 and had it certified on both sides of the Atlantic simultaneously. Apple got the iPod out in time for Christmas. Trust and flexibility are crucial, especially when decisions are being made while the product is undergoing development and testing. Successful organizations create cultures of trust and enable flexible networks that promote mutual understanding, rapid learning and the ability to change course quickly. Competitive advantage can be described as the ability to learn, innovate and reposition.

The creative process is usually an emotional one and all partnerships and relationships are by their nature messy. Alignment between parallel processes is enabled by efficient interaction, clear communication and trusting relationships. Often teams are spread across geographical areas and time zones. Networks of interpersonal relationships help make the difference between success and failure.

Successful organizations, programmes and projects need to work hard at enabling both the relationships and the communication required for success. The best managers actively design opportunities to do so.

As we move to a networked economy the concept of the linear supply chain has transformed into that of the non-linear value web. Successful organizations are able to identify the members of their value web and create opportunities where all these resources are working in harmony, and focused on a single goal – getting desirable products or services to market on time and on budget.

The companies that are most successful at mobilizing their value webs are those which engage in frequent interactions with their networks. How do you set up the preconditions to ensure you make the most of networks and enable teams to be successful?

FLEXIBILITY AND COMMUNICATION IN A VALUE WEB ARE DIRECTLY RELATED TO THE QUALITY OF INTERPERSONAL RELATIONSHIPS – ESTABLISH MULTIPLE OPPORTUNITIES FOR THESE TO DEVELOP

As a system moves through the cycles from innovation, proof of concept, piloting and testing to production and distribution, the types and qualities of teams change. These phases have their own distinct personalities and qualities and it takes a savvy manager to promote the context, attitude and environment that is required for each to be successful.

During innovation phases teams function best if they are:

- autonomous
- configured with the best members for the task
- connected to customers
- connected to your value web
- skilled in disciplines associated with innovation
- incentivized and measured

Each phase in the life cycle requires different skills moving from the unstructured to the structured. Even self-organizing teams need to recognize that the leaders of creative phases are usually different from the leaders of piloting, testing, production and distribution phases. However, despite changes of phase it is important that all teams keep checking in with customers and the entire value web. Rapid iterations and feedback cycles are best at all phases. Empowerment is vital – understand the acknowledged experts in the teams and let them make the decisions. Let packaging experts decided on packaging, let the logistics specialists decide on distribution, let designers make the design decisions. Flatten the hierarchies, and enable decision making.

CHECK IN WITH YOUR VALUE WEB

The opinions of your clients, employees, suppliers, customers and learning networks continue to be vital throughout the inexorable march to market. Encourage osmosis of ideas. In addition to generating ideas, you also begin to mobilize the users of the products, creating the buzz around the new products long before they are launched, and creating an influential user community in the process.

ITS technology demonstrates how working closely with your clients at the design stage ensures that you have an engaged set of clients before you enter production.

RAPID ITERATIONS AND FEEDBACK CYCLES

Creating opportunities for rapid iterations and feedback increases the sophistication of the product. IDEO create project spaces and displays for products in development that enable open feedback from all colleagues. The products are always visible, the teams are always in close proximity to each other. The same holds true for the design of services; process flows, video scenarios and use-case descriptions enable the communication of these ideas. Encourage teams to build formal and informal feedback cycles into their processes, throughout the life cycle of development and production.

EMPOWERMENT IS VITAL

Flattened hierarchies only work when roles are clear and everybody knows who takes responsibility for what. Making these roles visible helps. This is not to say that everybody is allowed an opinion on everything – the eureka moment may come from anywhere on a team! However, the final decision should rest with the expert on the team.

THE SERVING ROLE OF LEADERSHIP

The role of leadership within fast-moving, complex networks is to serve the teams' objective – through facilitation, arbitration and demonstration. Leaders are required to be sensitive to the changing moods of the network, to understand what blockages exist and to facilitate problem solving. Arbitration is vital when differences of opinion exist. Fundamentally, leaders model the behaviours they desire to encourage within the broader context of the programme.

ACKNOWLEDGE THE PROGRAMME PHASE

Sensitivity to the phase of the programme enables a large group to be clear about what needs to be done and who needs to take the lead. Film production is a powerful example of this because it is so visible. Studio time is costly, and everyone is aware of the phases of production – from filming, to editing, to screen testing and distribution. Acknowledge the programme phase and acknowledge the phase leader.

INCENTIVES AND MEASURES

Although teams need to be autonomous, it is important that members of the teams feel rewarded for the work they are doing. Most learning takes place in failure and the design process honours failure. High-volume, low-risk failure! However, business success is also a factor of time and budget – and incentives to meet these targets are vital. Measuring the success of teams against understood criteria, established clearly at the start, provides security. Getting things to market requires clear goals and deadlines. Healthy competition between teams allows the bar to be continuously raised in the areas of quality, outcome and sophistication. Teams find a sense of flow when they are challenged and tested in an environment which provides the skills necessary to achieve. All successful innovation, finally, is about people having fun.

Garrick Jones is a partner of the Ludic Group. He assists clients in building, equipping and launching the processes required for large-scale innovation environments. For the past seven years he has been a leader of Capgemini's Accelerated Solutions Environment and Innovate: UK. Having established the ASE in the UK he was involved in training teams and supporting centres around the world. In additional to his work for the Ludic Group, Garrick is a member of the extended network of IDEO, the industrial design group and is a visiting fellow at the London School of Economics (LSE) in the Institute of Social Psychology.

Further information: info@ludicgroup.com

2.6

Space for innovation

Fluid, flowing, spontaneous, random. David Leon at dlp,
a design and architecture consultancy, discusses workplaces
that inspire creativity

At the beginning of 2004 Her Majesty the Queen opened Oxford University's new £65 million Chemistry Laboratory.

Oxford University's Chemistry Department, the largest of its kind in the Western world and one of the most successful, is the owner of the new lab. The Department has a brilliant track record in spinning out new companies with novel innovations and taking a stake in their commercial successes. They are so successful, in fact, that they were able to fund a large part of the new laboratory through future earnings in their intellectual property.

When I went to see the new lab some months later, Professor Graham Richards, Chairman of the Chemistry Department and author of the new lab, told me: 'The new building has been influential in changing attitudes beyond our wildest dreams. Productivity has increased. Morale has gone sky high.'

My own experience is no different. My realization that the physical work-place is a factor in innovative performance began in 1988. Sir Geoffrey Allen, who was then Director of Research and Engineering at Unilever, put me in touch with the recently appointed Head of Laboratory at the company's Port Sunlight Laboratory. The brief was:

Internationalize the Port Sunlight Laboratory.
Release the creative talents of the staff.
Make technology respectable.

Internal research identified the factors that most affected these targets:

- the use of manpower;
- the use of time;
- the use of space.

The most surprising was the last. To cut a long story short, the Value Engineering Team re-engineered the organization. We were hired to redesign their workspace.

About 600 scientists and technicians occupied a large five-storey laboratory, built in the 1960s, with rows of enclosed laboratories and offices neatly laid out off long anonymous corridors. It was very depressing. You could walk along any of these drab corridors and never see another soul and never know where you were.

All the scientists sat in enclosed offices. You had to knock on the door to see if they were there. The technicians worked at solid teak benches in the labs beyond. Because there was so little storage for the equipment, glassware and samples, much of the bench space and fume cupboards became depositories.

Our solution to this was to knock out all the corridors and replace them with space-saving pull-out storage. We gave every scientist and technician their own work station alongside the lab benches so that everyone could get back to doing front-line science instead of writing reports – useful though those were.

The labs were open plan and, although some of the scientists were deeply suspicious at first, it enabled the interchange of ideas and promoted impromptu collaboration. We created little meeting and coffee areas with lots of whiteboards at various junctions and display areas for visitors – mostly from the Unilever businesses – to understand the work going on. We introduced different lighting and fresh new colour schemes, identities and signage.

The physical changes had to be phased over three years as the building was in constant occupation. Much to everyone's surprise, the first labs to be refurbished were a big success and after the initial culture shock departments queued up for the new treatment.

According to the head of the laboratory: 'The proportion of scientific time spent on actual research work as opposed to related activities increased dramatically because scientists were there in the labs – not hidden away in offices down the corridor.'

The businesses invested more because they could see better how research was supporting them. A third of the floor space was freed up for other purposes.

The building trade must be the most fragmented industry imaginable. This applies equally to the professions – architects, engineers, project managers, quantity surveyors, health and safety supervisors and many more – as it does to the building trades themselves. Many would argue – and I would agree with them – that as a consequence we are as an industry the least efficient and the least innovative, even though within our ranks there are numerous individual innovators.

When we designed a new Technical Centre for BP Chemicals at their new Business Park at Sunbury, UK, it was a BP requirement that we work from BP's own Site Project Office together with everyone else involved with developing the Park: project managers, engineers, cost engineers, contractors and suppliers – everyone.

Because we were all together in a single Project office several things happened:

- There was no doubt that the quality of problem solving was much higher than usual, leading to a better quality design solution. BP promoted a 'can do' culture to which we all subscribed.

- The design of the project was completed in 35 weeks instead of a standard 52 weeks – a deduction of 32 per cent, and our design costs were 30 per cent cheaper as a result.

- Construction took 54 weeks whereas it might have taken 70 weeks. Because we were there, problems could be resolved that afternoon – not the following week when we could find a convenient slot in our diaries.

Historically, building projects in commercial organizations fall under the responsibility of site engineers or estate managers. They see a building project only in terms of 'bricks and mortar'.

In contrast, space designed for innovation is a powerful management tool which can be engineered or re-engineered to optimize people performance. It is the glue that binds people, process and culture together. This can be achieved on an efficiency level, for example co-locating people who work together. It can equally be achieved on a behavioural level.

Environmental psychology as a social science is not so widely known in Europe and is given little more than lip service by the vast majority of architects or facilities managers. However, it examines the interrelationship between environments and human behaviour. It covers all aspects of life, from the impact of hospital design on patient recovery to the effect that deprived housing has on criminality.

Obviously, much work has been done on the study of the workplace. For those that remember, back in 1984, Tom Allen of MIT wrote a fascinating book on the topic entitled *Managing the Flow of Technology*. More recently, Tom Kelly's book *The Art of Innovation* addresses innovation and the work environment.

A powerful example of how the workplace influences behaviour is in Cincinnatti, Ohio. Procter & Gamble have a Fabric and Home Care Innovation Centre there. It has two wings, one on either side of railway lines, joined by a high-level walkway. One wing has been around for 50 years or so. It was planned in a conventional layout with individual offices off traditional corridors.

The other wing – The Millennium Wing – was designed in 2000 on entirely different principles, with large open-plan floors, dedicated project areas and a consumer lab – a fully working apartment where P&G scientists and consumers can undertake studies on new consumer products.

There cannot be a more perfect example of how two different work environments side by side for the same purpose impact so differently on people behaviour and as a result the success of innovation.

According to Dr Karl Ronn, the P&G Vice President responsible for the Centre, innovation is about what should be so that you can create something different.

Who knows who is going to have the solution to your problem? In the old building there is a formality and a lack of spontaneity. In the new building it is like walking through a garden – you can stop where you want.

Is creating the right workplace worth the cost? These are just a few of the comments by R&D directors of blue-chip global organizations about the impact of their new work environments on their people:

- ■ 'We have doubled our effectiveness in the three years that we have been here.'
- ■ 'This will provide an environment which encourages people to do science.'
- ■ 'A place where people can mix, interact and generate free flow of thought.'
- ■ 'Creates a new culture of openness and trust. Allows the business process to flow naturally. Stimulates synergy and interaction.'
- ■ 'Staff satisfaction rose to 96 per cent.'

For those who think the cost of change will be too much, facility costs are generally between 3 and 7 per cent of people costs calculated on the basis of net present value if you assume that the lifetime of a building is 20 years. In other words, if the facility cost is a mean average of 5 per cent you can cover the cost in a year. Is that too much for the obvious gains?

For those who think it is worth the cost, what are the key factors in the design of the work environment that will enhance creativity and innovation? Obviously, as can be seen from the BP example, co-location is essential. To be directly with the people of different disciplines you are working with on a project is a big asset.

As we work more globally this is not always possible. Technology, however, is advancing rapidly to solve the distance problem, with one-to-one video links, telephone conferencing and virtual workplaces. It will not be long before you can meet over a cup of coffee and be 3,000 miles away.

My view is, though, that however good the technology, it can only mitigate the problem of distance. There is no real substitute for physical co-location.

Another key factor is activity-based space. Walk into any office today and you will find it between 30 and 50 per cent empty. People are travelling or at meetings or maybe just on holiday. People have got used to working on planes, in hotel rooms and from their customers/suppliers/branch offices.

In this new mobile world the sterile argument of private offices versus open plan is no longer relevant. It is questionable if in some cases people need an office dedicated solely to them. Space for innovation is increasingly a range of discussion areas, meeting rooms, individual quiet and study areas. It is fluid and flowing and designed for spontaneity, random collisions and exchange of thoughts, ideas and gossip as well as private spaces for individual concentrated work.

Is it activity-based space?

- You can only have this fluidity if your IT and telephony are mobile.
- Infrastructures for unwired telephony and plug-in laptops are essential tools.
- Coupled with co-location and activity-based space is a need for transparency.
- Glass walls cost more than solid walls but it is vital that people are aware of what is going on.

As a nation here in the UK we are not very good at communication. Today, speed and accuracy demand that people be aware of, understand what is going on around them and communicate effectively.

A further key factor is flexibility. It is obvious to anyone in business today that the need for change does not diminish. It has taken on a life of its own. If we are going to stay co-located and move to satisfy yet another reorganization, we need an environment which is quick, easy and cheap to change. As someone at BP said to me, 'we are looking for the ten-minute, ten-dollar move'.

Another is functionality. At a personal level it is important. People want to do their job well. They have targets and deadlines to meet and I have never understood the habit of organizations not giving people the tools they need to do the job.

A lady in an HR department said to me recently that she had to get up and walk round several colleagues' desks to get to a printer 20 metres away. Every time she clicked 'print' on her computer and got up to get the paper copy she disturbed her colleagues, ran the risk of other people seeing confidential documents and got frustrated – all for the sake of a printer.

Finally, a healthy and safe environment is an essential feature of most modern workplaces. You cannot expect people to be on top form unless they have a healthy and safe place in which to work. This is easier said than done as buildings have become more sophisticated in their technology to provide an ever-increasing controlled environment.

The theory is fine but in reality many people find their place of work stuffy, either too hot or too cold, noisy and poorly lit. Many suffer from eyestrain, headaches, glare and tiredness and back problems. Not everyone complains but it is asking too much of people to be innovative if they are not feeling their best.

There is, however, a new enthusiasm to get back to basics, driven mostly by cost pressures, and to build workplaces which are energy efficient and healthy.

Space for innovation breaks with convention. Even though our working lifestyles have changed, most of us still work in formal layouts of office and lab space despite the fact that there is little proof that this convention is good for innovation.

Space designed for innovation, however, is fluid and informal, allowing people to work the way they want. It is space where furniture and equipment can be moved around at will and where people roam.

Naturally, as in any community, there have to be rules and at the end of the day people have to deliver the goods but if they are to do so they are entitled to the best tools available.

David Leon is head of dlp – a design and architecture consultancy he founded in the 1970s. The company specializes in designing work environments and buildings for innovation throughout Europe. These range across organizations in consumer goods, food and beverages, engineering, energy, chemicals and pharmaceuticals as well as academia.

Client organizations include BP, Borax, BNFL, Castrol, Coca-Cola, DSM, Dow Corning, Dana, Johnson & Johnson, Mercke Sharpe & Dohme, Novatis, Scott Bader, Smith & Nephew, Schlumberger, TWI, TU Delft and Unilever.

David has pioneered a unique design process which enables organizations to optimize performance through workplace design. Projects lead to both business performance gains and effective utilization of space.

David is a Member of the European Industrial Research Association (EIRMA), The UK R&D Society, the Environmental Design Research Association (EDRA) and is a Fellow of the Chartered Society of Designers. He is also a Fellow of the Royal Society of Arts. He writes and lectures extensively on the Innovation Workplace. Tel: 00 44 20 7223 0308; Fax: 0044 20 7223 0401; e-mail: david.leon@dlp.co.uk; web: www.dlp.co.uk.

Accelerated solutions

The Accelerated Solutions Enviroment, which combines the features of a theatre and a production studio, enables complex teams to come up with new ideas and put them into production, says Garrick Jones of the Ludic Group.

The nature of work is changing rapidly and project work is becoming the norm. Most innovation and production is project led, powered by workshops, and the benefits are often difficult to quantify. This is as true for aircraft production as it is for the development of new derivative products for banking. The loss of proximity to team-mates is another difficulty, as teams may be working on components of a solution across geographic and temporal boundaries. Given that the time that teams are able to spend together is precious, how can the most be made of those interactions? How can we ensure that the work we do together, rapidly achieves quality outcomes? That the value of working together more than outweighs the cost of bringing people together? How can we guarantee creativity from very large groups? One response to meeting these complex business needs is the Accelerated Solutions Environment (ASE™) and Innovate: UK that was developed for the consulting firm of Ernst & Young and bought, in turn, by Cap Gemini.

A PHYSICAL ENVIRONMENT

Imagine an environment full of toys and puzzles, books and workstations, a theatre for large group work, as well as smaller spaces to work individually or in teams. Imagine that it is possible to draw on the walls, and that there exists a team of people who are dedicated to capturing everything you produce and placing it in an easy-to-access web tool, seconds after you have produced it. Imagine that the web knowledge base contains access to databases that are useful to the work you are doing. Imagine an environment in which everything is on wheels – including the plants. It contains plasma screens and computers, a matrix of electrical and audio visual sub-systems in order to permit its communication systems to be configured in any way conceivable. A place where large groups from 50 to 250 can interact, design, develop, prototype and produce in a carefully constructed, highly supportive environment. This is the concept behind accelerated solutions: to ensure that when large groups get together, the experience is creative, useful and enjoyable. Where film-making has pre-production, production and post-production facilities, so too does the innovation industry.

A VIRTUAL KNOWLEDGE ENVIRONMENT

Any commercial context contains a wealth of information. Such a database exists physically, virtually and socially, both within heads and within groups or teams.

Paying attention to the knowledge environment in which a group finds itself, enables more powerful decision making. A support crew capturing all the information generated by participants through video, sound, drawing and the web makes this knowledge base available to participants seconds after its creation. This enables new ideas, models, plans, visions, and prototypes to be used as powerful resources.

The capture and display of information in multiple formats provides instantaneous feedback to large groups. Through a process of ever-increasing cycles of feedback, a group is able to navigate its way through the labyrinth of information.

Providing documentation and knowledge bases for large groups as they move through cycles of creativity, design and production creates two important things: a narrative of the journey of their development, and a catalogue of the end product and the iterations that were needed to achieve it.

Beyond the design event, these records become powerful learning tools for the implementation programmes coming after. They also provide context-rich records, which provide those joining the teams later in the cycle with a clear record of what's been going on.

ACTIVATING PROCESSES

When a disparate group comes together, how is it possible to get rapidly down to work as a fully functional team?

Time is vital. To work together in a high-powered way is probably not going to take place in a day – unless the team has experienced that way of working before. It takes three or four days of hard work for groups to get to a point where they can achieve powerful results quickly.

Processes that enable large groups to explore and understand what they are dealing with need to be challenging. Groups need powerful tools to explore, model, and communicate ideas. One way of understanding the complexity of an idea is by approaching it using as many different learning states as possible. One useful system is Howard Gardner's centre of intelligence model, which includes the kinaesthetic, linguistic, mathematical, logical, interpersonal, intra-personal, musical and intuitive.

Accelerated solutions uses a creative process approach which works through cycles of identity, vision, intent, insight, engineering, building and using to enable decision making based on rapid feedback and broad contextual understanding. It is probably best known for the Scan, Focus, Act model which creates distinct phases for the development of ideas.

Accelerated solutions is about connecting the team with information, design resources, creative processes and communication media in a manner that enables four things: a deep understanding of the landscape of information, critical exploration of alternatives and problem solving, prototyping and simulation; and tools for communicating decisions made – all of this in a highly configured, fun and useful environment. Such workspaces are vital for addressing the challenges of time, proximity, creativity, scale and cost. It is a production studio and a theatre for the networked, knowledge economy – spaces which quickly move ideas from feeling to action.

Garrick Jones is a partner of the Ludic Group. He assists clients in building, equipping and launching the processes required for large-scale innovation environments. For the past seven years he has been a leader of Cap Gemini's Accelerated Solutions Environment and Innovate: UK. Having established the ASE in the UK he was involved in training teams and supporting centres around the world. In addition to his work for the Ludic Group, Garrick is a member of the extended network of IDEO, the industrial design group and is a visiting fellow at the London School of Economics (LSE) in the Institute of Social Psychology.

Further information: info@ludicgroup.com

2.8

Fast-tracking the commercialization of intellectual property

The process of commercially managing innovations is in general disastrously handled, says Billy Harkin

'Innovation and how to manage it' is about as easy to define and collectively agree on, as is say 'how to find love' and 'how to let it flourish', ie damned near impossible to agree on. And therein lies the problem – and the main reason that only a tiny proportion of innovations ever see the light of day as real products and services; and an even smaller proportion ever see commercial success. We currently have no agreed definition for innovation and we have no agreed method of commercially managing innovation.

With the formal system of protecting innovation (intellectual property rights) having been with us for over 300 years now (thanks to those clever Venetians), it really is high time that we got our acts together re practical systems of capitalizing on the intellectual property rights (IPRs) that are created.

The cop-out to date has, I suggest, been largely along the lines of 'but *innovation* means many things to many people, it's a *creative process* that cannot be bounded, nor systematically managed'. To which I say 'baloney!' And that until we do collectively agree on particular categorizations of innovation – and then all work collaboratively together within those understood parameters – we will continue to spend more time debating innovation than actually delivering tangible outputs that serve any useful purpose.

To cut through the debate then, allow me to offer some of my own crude but time-served categorization, if I may. Let's take innovation as having five distinct flavours:

1. an innovative *thought* – that leads to some *expressible work of art* – of *aesthetic value* alone;

2. an innovative *thought* – that leads to some new *philosophical perspective;*

3. an innovative *thought* – that leads to some *new process* (that can achieve something already well known, but achieves it better, faster or cheaper than via pre-existing processes);

4. an innovative *thought* – that leads to some new *service or services;*

5. an innovative *thought* – that leads to some new *product or products.*

Much time is spent debating the approaches to, and the merits of, items 1, 2, 3 and 4. No more will be spent here. Not because they don't have merit, but simply because my own past 25 years of experience have been immersed solely in the area of item 5. And in particular on how to approach systematically capitalizing on the commercially useful innovations and efficiently abandoning the ones that are not.

Mankind has creatively spewed a barrage of innovative thoughts since Adam and Eve (or since 'the big bang', depending on your preference). The process of generating 'innovations' works well, almost effortlessly well – in fact for lots of people it's hard to stop having innovative thoughts and accumulating new ideas. However, the process of commercially managing those innovations has always been, and remains in general, disastrously badly handled.

Figure 2.8 shows the entire commercial management process in context, within which there is a clear process for exploiting IPR, from the point of its invention all the way through to the delivery of real products – these resultant products being produced either by a newly established company built for the purpose, or alternatively by existing companies that have been granted the licence rights to do so.

The methodology of the exploitation process – the '5 Star IPR-commercialization process' – has been encapsulated within an ASP application (EIPAM™) as a practical project management tool for those involved in the

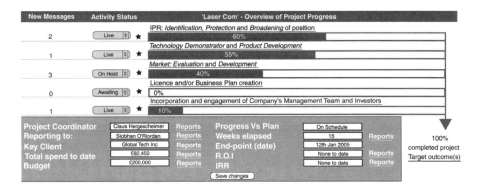

Figure 2.8: *Commercial management process*

innovation business, including inventors, licensing executives and technology transfer managers. The collaborative environment ensures that all others required within the innovation-management mix – patent agents, product designers, marketing and finance people etc – are also actively coordinated towards the declared common goal.

The EIPAM™ tool and its process includes all the critical activities related to validating the commercial potential of an IPR-based innovation, first proving the technology concept, then systematically advancing in practical steps towards licensing or creating new ventures to bring products to market. The nature of the IPR within a given project will of course determine the nature of the products emerging from that project – eg a medical device, a domestic product, some software, or perhaps even a movie or a book. The tool with its clearly defined activities helps guide the user to expedite the exploitation process.

It is beyond the scope of this short chapter to describe the nitty-gritty of the detail of the average number of 80 activities and contracts associated with the process, as used for industrial and consumer product outputs. Accessed through a standard web browser, all documents, reports and e-mails, decision taking etc are actively managed from start to finish – a clear unified project management with full audit trail results. Users can either utilize a pre-loaded set of style guides, or can default-load their own, as long as the insertion of their own style guides maintains the overall quality and efficiency of the '5 Star IPR-commercialization' final output.

Nothing about the approach is 'rocket science' as they say – simply a ruthlessly organized and driving approach to dismissing the majority of innovations (as being commercially useless) and allowing concentration on speeding the production and profitable sale of the innovations that have been realistically filtered and organized to have the best chance of success in the market.

SUMMARY

If your focus is to make money out of an innovative thought, then focus on the production of real products, real processes and real services – and on producing them as quickly as possible at the lowest possible cost; and on then selling them for profit.

Stating the obvious, this is *not*. The intoxicating process of innovation itself, combined with really bad commercial management, routinely sends the vast majority of innovative and 'could-have-been-valuable' projects over an expensive cliff!

Managing the multidisciplinary, multifaceted process of turning IPR from a spend activity into a profitable one is tough, but can be professionally managed. Get organized. Unashamed recommendation: buy EIPAM™ – the world's first invention for managing inventions – and use it mercilessly.

Alternatively, organize your own ('uninfringing' of course) 'methodology and collaborative-management environment'. But either way, get organized and manage the damn process ... rather than letting *it* manage you!

In January 2002, Billy and colleagues formed Science Ventures – a specialist science and technology sector IPR-commercialization company to serve the 'University and Research Institute' sector and Corporate sector in the UK. He has also established two other companies within the past 12 months. IPCI Ltd (Intellectual Property Commercialization Institute) is a practical IPR commercialization skills training company designed to up-skill both public and private sector personnel directly involved in, or associated supporters of, the commercialization of IPR assets. Projected Outcome Ltd (POL), where he serves as chairman, is an enterprise solutions software company that offers integrated project management and document management solutions, including one particular application, EIPAM™ (incorporating the '5 Star IPR-commercialization process').

For the previous four years, he was Head of Technology Transfer at Glasgow University, where over the next four years he recruited, trained and led a team that commercialized the IPR assets of the University. Successes included Kymata Ltd, the fastest-growth university spin-out company in terms of market value and number of employees hired. Within two years Kymata grew to a value of $1 billion and *employed 540 staff. With a change in the technology market, it was successfully sold to Alcatel. Ten other spin-out launches and a selection of licence deals followed.*

Billy is a regular guest speaker at IPR-commercialization conferences around the world and has presented in the United States, South Africa, France, Ireland, Japan and throughout the UK.

Contact: Billy Harkin, Chairman, Projected Outcome Ltd at bharkin@projected-outcome.com

2.9

Technology transfer

Unless technology is packaged in a way that is appropriate and easily understood, the original idea is sure to fail, argues Paul Pankhurst at Carbonate

Sound intellectual property is just part of the mix required for successful exploitation. Understanding the external conditions such as the end user, the route to market and the key partners that have to be engaged along the way is critical from the outset.

It is important to acknowledge that the intellectual property (IP) at the start of the innovation process may be different from the IP at the end, as user needs and market conditions shape the final solution.

To be successful throughout the process, design and communication are all-important. Unless the technology is packaged in a way that is appropriate and easily understood – reflecting customer needs and meeting partners' commercial expectations – the original idea is sure to fail.

Most businesses are aware of the importance of innovation as a vital ingredient for competitiveness, productivity and future growth; it is a universally accepted truth that innovation = the successful exploitation of new ideas.

While technical brilliance and original insight might give birth to new ideas and opportunities, unless you can translate that technology or concept into a commercially viable and marketable opportunity, your patent certificates will do nothing other than gather dust! You will have relinquished your thoughts to the public domain and, worse still, your competitors.

Successful technology transfer is the key to commercial success.

TECHNOLOGY TRANSFER IN THE INNOVATION PROCESS

There are a number of critical elements to technology transfer in the innovation process:

- *Identify/develop technology.* Clearly this is a fundamental building block. However, technical viability and market acceptability may be unclear at this early stage.

- *Seek protection.* Much has been said on when you should seek protection. There is a balance between disclosing too early, while the idea is still embryonic and subject to change, and too late, when others file a similar solution. Early investment in protection allows engagement with key partners (under confidentiality) to better determine commercial viability.

- *Secure funding (IP, design/development, production, distribution, sales and marketing).* Underestimating the multi-level skills and investment in time and money required to take the initial idea through to commercial reality is a common occurrence. It is possible to break down the funding required to cover each step of the process and negotiate staged cash injections against certain milestones being reached, but remember that you need to keep convincing investors that the idea is gaining value. If you underestimate the task and need to secure additional funding it will almost certainly be expensive money. Be prepared to let go – recognize your key strengths and recruit or partner with others to help you commercialize.

- *Develop appropriate solution to user need/want.* Technologies and ideas evolve. Being objective and receptive to change is important. Listen to the market – seek insights from consumer behaviour. Check that your idea addresses a problem that isn't already solved by other means. Check this on a global scale.

- *Develop route to market.* Route to market dynamics can be extremely complex even for the most simple of ideas. Being able to think big and strategic as opposed to tactical and opportunistic will deliver better long-term returns.

- *Approach and engage partners (networking – especially global contacts – PDD).* Professionalism is a prerequisite. More often than not, you only get one shot at partner engagements, so the approach has to be considered, the material compelling and recognition that you are selling and your partner is buying into your idea. No one likes a pushy sales representative with a fixed viewpoint and only one thing to sell!

- *Negotiate licences.* This can be a long and complex task. The most difficult component to predict when getting a product to market is the time it will take. Many ventures fail, not because of the product or its suitability for the market, but an underestimate of the time it takes to get to revenue by which time the finances are exhausted. Be prepared, and seek commercial and legal advice along the way.

- *Embody technology (storyboards, working rigs, prototypes, concepts).* Design and packaging of the technology will accelerate the comprehension of the commercial partners and increase the likelihood of adoption.

- *Communicate technology (2D/3D, mixed media).* Use the most appropriate media for the audience and work the key messages. First impressions count.

TURNING IDEAS INTO BUSINESS

At Carbonate, rarely is an idea submitted to us that is 100 per cent ready for market. Frequently the output during the process from idea to commercial success is somewhat different from the input.

Carbonate has been involved in a number of successful commercializations where it has been necessary to adapt and change the original idea based on a range of external factors that became apparent during the commercialization process.

An example is 'Duality' – a multiple-fragrance air freshener. The original idea was that of cycling through a number of fragrances to avoid the monotony of a single fragrance using heated gels. Today, Duality delivers two different yet complementary liquid scents from perfume-styled bottles at timed intervals to overcome olfactory fatigue. Carbonate partnered with a flavour and fragrance designer and manufacturer to optimize fragrance performance and user experience. Working prototypes were independently tested for fragrance impact, longevity and combination both in development and with end users.

Table 2.9(i) shows how, through the process, the original idea has evolved.

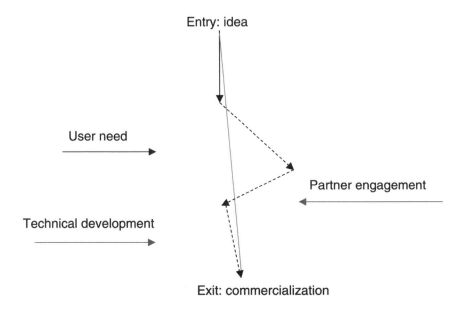

Figure 2.9 (i)   *Influences on an idea*

Example 1: Duality

The original idea evolved from rough sketches through working prototypes demonstrating the effect of switching fragrances and 2D artist's sketches for market feedback. Partner engagement was most effective, with clear planning, market knowledge and technology positioning using focused presentation materials, operational prototypes and the 2D visuals.

Example 2: the DECK

The DECK is a reconfigurable exercise platform, the brainchild of Loughborough University spin-out Progressive Sports Technologies Ltd (PSTL). Here again the original idea, despite being conceptually sound, was in no shape to be taken directly to prospective manufacturing and distribution partners as they would not be able to envisage in an initial presentation meeting what the consumer product could look like. With emphasis placed on gathering user and market understanding, the original idea evolved and through design and carefully targeted communication the commercialization process was accelerated. Successful engagement of targeted brand partners was made possible through well-developed prototypes and clear, well-developed business propositions.

Table 2.9 (i)   Duality – Dual Fragrance air freshener

Idea Input	Value add	Output
Multiple fragrance	Tech: Only 2 fragrances required	
	Mkt: Trend in dual (mixed) scents	Duality – dual
Heated gel	Tech: Gel ineffective in delivering high impact	fragrance
	Forced air proven to be more effective than heat at fragrance dispersal	Oil-based
	Mkt: Trend away from gels, towards essential oils	fragrances
Battery powered	Tech: Power insufficient to deliver required duration	
	Mkt: Typical user not technophile; green issues around use of batteries	Plug-in device
Sachet fragrance	Tech: Insufficient fragrance for duration	Glass bottles with coloured
	Mkt: No visible user appeal/ communication	fragrances

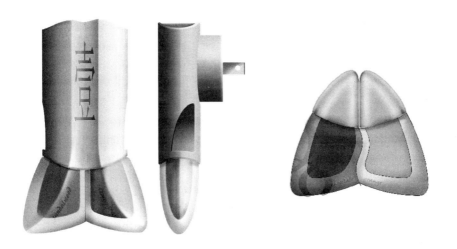

Figure 2.9 (ii)   *Duality – 2-D marketing visuals*

Table 2.9 (ii)   The Reebok Deck – Exercise platform

Idea Input	Value add	Output
LEGO block concept	Reconfiguration counter-intuitive	Easy-to-understand sun-lounger design
	Difficult to stack – many parts	One part
	Reconfiguration time consuming	Quick to change
	Difficult to see how the product could be rationalized into a consumer product	Product styling creates a need for ownership

Communication: a highly-emotive 3-minute film which describes, by way of example, the various work-out routines that can be performed. The film includes a look-alike semi-functional model of the proposed product.

HOW DO WE DO IT?

Our Innovation Process is important to ensure a balanced and impartial approach; the gates (0–6) act as 'sanity checks' conducted by experts in engineering, consumer understanding, marketing and business planning. A project champion, who has ownership of the idea, maintains momentum. It allows Carbonate to engage consistently with both innovators and commercial

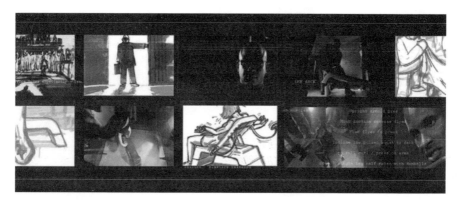

Figure 2.9 (iii)   *The Reebok Deck – Storyboard for videos*

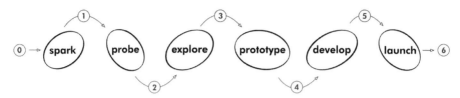

Figure 2.9 (iv)   *Carbonate innovation stages and gates*

partners. At each stage there are different deliverables and entry/exit conditions. For example, in Probe, technical feasibility is determined in terms of performance and cost. Qualitative and quantitative research defines the size of the opportunity and the routes to market. A business case is constructed and the decision as to whether the project should continue is made.

CONCLUSION

Technical transfer in the Innovation Process needs to engage with the user, the market and relevant commercial partners. Willingness to adapt to meet those needs and using design and a variety of communication techniques will both accelerate and increase the likelihood of commercial success.

Carbonate Ltd is a spin-out company from the UK's largest product design consultancy, PDD Ltd. Carbonate has established a process and track record for innovating and licensing new products, capitalizing on the wealth of experience and facilities within PDD. Carbonate enjoys a unique relationship with PDD through which professional contacts, product development experience and know-how may be leveraged.

Carbonate adds value in the form of user understanding and design to create a compelling product proposition and negotiates licensing deals on behalf of the idea originator. The vibrant, inventive culture focuses on the evaluation and development of product opportunities, building strategic partnerships and the development of successful commercial propositions.

Contact details: Carbonate Ltd, 85 Richford Street, London W6 7HJ; Tel: +44 (0)20 8735 1199; Fax: +44 (0)20 8735 1188; e-mail: info@carbonate.co.uk; web: www.carbonate.co.uk.

2.10

R&D tax credits

Have you claimed your research and development tax credits,
ask David O'Keeffe and David Bywater at KPMG

It's not just men and women in white coats who do research and development!

The research and development (R&D) tax credits are available to companies undertaking a far wider range of activities than most people think. Some companies are therefore failing to claim the relief to which they are entitled, while others are sometimes not claiming all that they could.

INTRODUCTION

In April 2000 R&D tax credits were introduced for small and medium-sized companies (SMEs). A similar relief was introduced from April 2002 for large companies. These incentives were aimed at encouraging those companies involved in the cycle of innovation, ranging from early-stage research through to specific product development.

The mechanics of the respective tax incentives are in theory straightforward. However, when working through the process of preparing a claim, the following key areas need to be understood:

- the actual rules which govern the R&D tax credits for SMEs and large companies, respectively;
- the definition of R&D for tax purposes;
- the categories of expenditure which are eligible for relief;
- how a claim should be prepared and presented to the Inland Revenue.

Each of these points is covered in turn below.

R&D TAX CREDITS – THE KEY LEGISLATIVE PROVISIONS

While the regimes for SMEs and large companies have many similarities, there are some fundamental differences. In practice, the regime for SMEs is aimed at rewarding companies that bear the financial cost of the R&D, whereas the large-company scheme rewards companies that actually undertake the R&D irrespective of who bears the financial cost. Table 2.10(i) sets out the key principles underlying each regime.

As with most tax legislation, there are some more complex provisions, but these are outside of the scope of this chapter. Companies should therefore seek professional advice on this subject.

WHAT ACTIVITIES QUALIFY AS R&D?

The definition of R&D for these purposes is now set out in the Guidelines issued by the DTI in March 2004. These guidelines give several examples of the types of development activities which could qualify, including:

- extending the overall knowledge or capability in a field of science or technology;
- making an appreciable (non-trivial) improvement to an existing product or process; or
- developing a product with the same performance characteristics as existing models, but which is built in a fundamentally different manner, eg a 'cost-down' development project.

This new definition provides considerable scope to claim for activities ranging from research to the development of new or improved products. For

Table 2.10 (i)   Key principles

Key principles	SME regime	Large-company regime
Categorization	A company is an SME[1] if: ■ Number of employees <250; and ■ Turnover ≤€40m or balance sheet total ≤€27m; and ■ 25% or more of the company's capital or voting rights are not owned by an enterprise which itself is not an SME. (There are limited exceptions to this condition)	Any company that is not an SME
Commencement date	Relief available for expenditure incurred from 1 April 2000	Relief available for expenditure incurred from 1 April 2002
Requirements as regards any intellectual property generated by the R&D	The IP must initially vest, whether solely or jointly, with the claimant company	There is no requirement for the IP to vest with the claimant company
Contracted-in R&D	A company cannot claim for activities which are contracted to it by another party. (There are special rules which allow an SME to claim the large-company relief if the contractor is, for instance, a large company)	The company can generally claim for activities which are contracted to it by another party
Subsidies or contributions against the expenditure	The quantum of the claim is reduced to the net cost to the company. (If the subsidy is notified state aid, such as a DTI Smart Award, then no claim can be made against that particular project)	Subsidies and contributions have no effect on the quantum of the claim, i.e. the company can claim for its gross qualifying costs ignoring any contributions received against this expenditure

[1]For accounting periods ending on or after 1 January 2005, an updated SME definition applies; the turnover and balance sheet total thresholds are increased to €50m and €43m respectively. The independence test has been replaced with more complex rules, outside of the scope of this article, which apply when calculating whether a company which has 'linked' and 'partner' enterprises falls within the employee and financial thresholds.

instance, we have made claims for companies involved in activities ranging from the research and product development of new technologies for wireless internet connection through to the design and development of a new range of heavy lifting forklift trucks.

QUALIFYING EXPENDITURE

The categories of expenditure that can be claimed under the two regimes are broadly the same, with one fundamental difference relating to the treatment of sub-contract costs. Qualifying expenditure is defined to include:

1. The staff costs of employees undertaking the R&D activities, including now a proportion of the costs paid for agency staff.
2. Some of the expenditure incurred in subcontracting R&D to third parties. In general, SMEs can include in their claim 65 per cent of the amount paid to subcontractors. Large companies, on the other hand, cannot claim for amounts paid to subcontractors, subject to the limited exceptions where the subcontractor is a specific type of entity such as a university.
3. The costs of materials and expendable equipment used up in the R&D process, which for large companies includes, from 1 April 2004, software directly used in the R&D and expenditure on the utilities consumed on R&D. For SMEs the relevant date will be that on which approval is given by the European Commission.

The R&D tax credits are not given on capital expenditure. Instead, capital expenditure incurred on R&D should qualify for another tax incentive for R&D, being the 100 per cent capital allowances.

VALUE OF THE INCENTIVES

R&D credits are given by allowing a 'super deduction' in calculating taxable profits. For SMEs the deduction is equal to 150 per cent of the qualifying expenditure, whereas for large companies the deduction is 125 per cent. There are also provisions to allow loss-making SMEs to claim a cash repayment from the Inland Revenue; these provisions do not extend to the large-company scheme.

Table 2.10 (ii)   R & D expenditure

For £500k of R&D expenditure	SME scheme	Large-company scheme
Super deduction	£250k (plus normal deduction of £500k)	£125k (plus normal deduction of £500k)
Tax saving at 30%	£75k (plus normal tax relief of £150k)	£37.5k (plus normal tax relief of £150k)
Repayable tax credit if loss making	£120k (capped at total PAYE/NIC paid by the company in the period)	

OPTIMIZING THE RELIEF

There is no shortcut to making a claim which both optimizes the level of relief and also stands up to the scrutiny of the Tax Inspector. In summary, the following broad approach should be followed in compiling a claim:

- The starting point is to analyse the activities in the company, including the less obvious areas, to identify which fall within the definition of R&D.

- A methodology should be designed to capture all of the eligible expenditure attaching to those activities identified as R&D. There should be procedures to identify all of the staff involved in the R&D, and also to quantify the proportion of their time spent on the qualifying projects. This can be relatively straightforward in some instances, but for large companies with R&D activities spread across several functions this can be more complex.

- The relevant non-staff costs also need to be captured. This could perhaps be done via a review of the expense codes or via a more sophisticated system which automatically identifies and extracts the appropriate expenditure from the accounting systems.

- The actual claim will normally be included in the annual corporation tax return. The Inland Revenue have stated that the information which they expect to see is an analysis of the expenditure claimed together with a 'brief synopsis, in layman's terms, of the activities (being claimed) and the basis on which they constitute R&D'. If such supporting information is not provided, the tax inspector will invariably ask for it.

The time limit for making claims is six years from the end of the relevant accounting period. This period is reduced to two years if the claim is for the cash-back alternative by an SME. Hence, it is possible to revisit old years and make retrospective claims, subject of course to the time limits and the actual commencement dates of 1 April 2000 and 1 April 2002 respectively.

SUMMARY

The key message is that R&D tax credits are available on a wider range of activities than most people initially think. Companies should therefore consider carefully whether they have activities that could potentially qualify for relief, and if necessary take the appropriate professional advice. Failure to do so could result in a lost opportunity.

The value of the relief can be significant. Companies that qualify for the incentive should therefore ensure that they optimize their first claim, and then implement procedures that facilitate the preparation of future claims. This should then provide a year-on-year benefit.

David O'Keeffe is the Partner who heads KPMG's Research and Development Tax Relief Group, and David Bywater is a Senior Manager in the Group. Both have specialized in advising on the tax incentives for R&D since their introduction in the UK, and both have also worked with various trade organizations, and in consultation with the government, in connection with the initial construction and subsequent changes to the schemes.

Part 3

Inventive marketing

Markets planning

Enthusiasm can easily lead to misplaced assumptions, says Dr Shailendra Vyakarnam at Cambridge University's Judge Institute of Management. First be clear about the size and dynamics of the market and then decide on the right business model

In order to clarify the opportunity and prepare to write a plan, you will need to cover a certain amount of ground by way of research and discussions with your team. It is essential that your personal values and the assumptions you are making about the marketplace, customers, technology, legal and regulatory constraints are made clear and transparent before you embark on the tough process of writing a plan and starting to market the opportunity to others.

The MARKETS approach is a thinking tool and is an iterative process, building on an increasing level of understanding of:

M – **Markets**	The specific and general needs of the marketplace.
A – **Approach**	How you will commercialize the idea.
R – **Returns**	Thinking about the rewards and risks in the business and how the shareholders and managers will be rewarded for the effort.

K – **Knowledge**   What is the uniqueness of the business? Can it be protected in some way through patents, copyrights and trademarks? How will knowledge be renewed?

E – **Ethics**   Do the ethics of the team and the business and/or industry align comfortably with each other?

T – **Teams**   What are the skills, resources and capabilities of the top team like and can the team function well, with shared values and vision?

S – **Sustainability**   Thinking through the long-term sustainability of the business in order to compete effectively.

The rest of this article focuses on what you need to think about with markets, the approach you take to commercialization and how you will be sustainable. A full version of the article is downloadable from www.transitions. co.uk/downloads.

MARKETS

What is the basic unmet need you are trying to fill? Is this unmet need sufficiently large to provide for a big enough and growing market to make it worth while starting a business or launching your product? Think through from a generic definition of the market to identify segments that you can think of as customers who will buy from you, and why they might do so.

All projects must be driven from a thorough understanding of the needs, namely: *specific needs* that the business is addressing; *general needs* to which the business relates and which set the context – these may affect how the specific needs evolve and may also lead to follow-on opportunities.

Questions relating to the *specific needs* include the following:

- Who are the customers? What problems do they have?
- How serious is the need and why? Is it a need or just a 'nice to have'? Will it endure or could it fade away? What is the urgency?
- If there are several aspects to the need, what is most important? Where could the greatest value be created by a good solution?
- What constrains how any solution will be accepted and used? What is needed in order to fit with existing standards, practices, infrastructure, products, assumptions, and culture? What is needed to achieve easy adoption and use?

■ Is a technology solution needed? For example, could the problem be solved by legal, social or legislative means? To what extent is a 'soft solution' or whole life support needed alongside any technology solution?

Questions relating to the *general needs* include the following:

■ To what extent are the specific needs a subset of wider and longer-term problems, concerns or opportunities? How far, by addressing the specific needs, can we position ourselves to address the more general needs? How might the technology, product or service be reused for other offerings?

■ Can we foresee how these general needs will develop? How might this increase or decrease the specific needs?

■ What assumptions underpin our analysis of the specific needs? What events or changes could substantially alter these needs? How likely are they to happen? What do we need to watch?

■ Where are the needs most acute and/or growing rapidly? How important are they in the UK?

There is always a danger of 'pushing' an existing technology solution instead of focusing on what is really needed. Therefore care must be taken that the analysis of specific needs is done objectively, without being distorted by personal enthusiasms or what you want to sell or develop. The analysis must be well informed by information from customers and those who know the market and customers well.

It is sometimes true that customers do not know they need a product until they see it, but we need to recognize clearly if we are making a leap of faith about the needs. It may be that we have a leading position in some radically new technology for which it is not possible to foresee all of the applications. But it is essential to identify what can provide the initial market and the revenue for exploiting other opportunities as they become clearer.

The analysis of needs should include a preliminary quantification of the value proposition in financial terms:

■ How much is the output worth to customers and what are they likely to pay?

■ What is the benefit through preventing loss of life, waste of time or resources, loss of output, financial loss, poor decisions...?

In putting together the information and assumptions about customers' needs and the size and dynamics of the marketplace you can then begin to think about the approach you will take to enter the market – the business model you need to maximize your opportunity.

APPROACH

What is the approach you will take to meeting this need and how will you turn the opportunity into revenues and profits? You will need to address the business strategy and the business model at this stage. For example, do you need to start a business or should you license your idea or create a joint venture?

The analysis of the approach starts from imagining ways to meet the needs or solve the problems, and then, hopefully, leads to one or more compelling approach(es) and to an identified team and plan for undertaking the project if it goes ahead.

Many ideas should be examined. From the perspective of technical and commercial assurance, what is important is evidence that sufficient effort, breadth of expertise and imagination have been devoted to ideas generation and thinking about risks, to be reasonably confident that there are no compelling approaches, serious unknowns or major risks that have been missed. There are many methods that can be used for creating ideas, including tools that support lateral thinking and networking.

The same methods of brainstorming and group discovery can also be used for discovering risks and uncertainties.

A compelling approach should score well against the following questions:

- How new and inventive is the approach? Is it likely to lead to valuable intellectual property that can be patented or otherwise protected?

- How effective is the approach? Does it meet the needs perfectly or only partially? Is it focused on meeting the needs, free of unnecessary novelty, risk, elaboration and complexity?

- How unique is the approach in meeting the need? Could it easily be overtaken by a competitive approach? Is the approach special or one of many approaches of comparable merit?

- How clever is the approach? Will the cleverness appeal to customers? Will the cleverness enhance our reputation? Will the cleverness make the approach easy to defend against competitors?

■ Very important, do we have validated confidence that the approach will work technically? Could the novelty or complexity add major risk (eg might software implementation have unacceptable problems)?

Opportunity cost is another important consideration. If a project uses all the best people, this will prevent other opportunities being exploited. Therefore the team must make appropriately frugal use of the best talent, choosing wisely in exploiting resources from outside the business.

Financial frugality and a focus on the key uncertainties are also highly important. The project should start lean and focus on reducing the key uncertainties, at each stage avoiding work that is not yet necessary. This is important not only for husbanding the financial resources but also so that other activities do not divert attention away from what really matters. Often there are cheap routes to reduce the uncertainties, through using outside experts and simple prototypes. Maintaining a risk register is a good way to ensure a disciplined focus on the key uncertainties.

This kind of analysis will then help you to steer towards a decision about whether you should:

■ **Sell the idea/patent** to someone else because the nature of your idea is better exploited by someone else. There are advantages and disadvantages to this approach, mainly that you pass on your idea to someone else, for which you will be paid upfront, but you give up future potential revenue streams.

■ **License** the idea to a partner organization. There are many forms of licence arrangements in which you can benefit from royalty streams and have continued involvement (as agreed), but you will rely on the partner organization for the overall exploitation of the idea.

■ **Joint venture or partnership** arrangements can be developed where each partner brings something to the deal and has identifiable benefits. This can be complex to set up, needs partners with unique advantages and can be rewarding in the long term.

■ **Make and sell**. This is where the entrepreneur/inventor or the business decides to make and sell the product, being in full control of all the production, distribution and sales. The benefits are clearly that a new venture is created with all the upside benefits but carrying all the risks too. The firm has to possess all the resources and management capability to be successful with this strategy.

SUSTAINABILITY

The analysis of sustainability involves: assessing who the competitors are likely to be, what they are likely to offer, what competitive advantages they may have, what competitive advantage you have and how to maximize this. Price may be an important factor. So may be the capability to make an excellent proposal and presentation to customers.

Sustaining the competitive advantage is also a critical issue, both for an existing business or offering, and for a new venture. Generally, unless there is a formidable *barrier to entry*, the more successful a business is the more likely it is to attract competitors. Therefore, even if there are no competitors now, they are likely to emerge if the business is successful.

The questions in *assessing sustainable competitive advantage* include:

- Who are the existing competitors and how well established are they?

- What is our competitive advantage in terms of: patents, partnerships, technical ability and know-how, share of the market, facilities, de facto standards, and reputation? How does this compare with our competitors?

- What gives the most competitive advantage in the venture? How strong is it? In what part of the value chain does it lie? Does its sustainability depend on our business, or on one of our partners in the venture?

- How strong is our patent portfolio? What would it take to prosecute the patents?

- If the venture is based strongly on technology know-how, do we own all of the core know-how and patents? Would we have to reinvent someone else's knowledge, or get round their patents, now or in the future?

- How do we avoid losing our know-how lead through competitors recruiting our staff?

- Can we codify the knowledge to protect ourselves against losing a key person?

- Where are our competitors currently investing, and are any of them likely to invest in direct competition to our investment?

- Is the market expanding so fast that there is room for everyone, or will competition be intense?

- If our advantage is based on lead-time, do we have a meaningful head start and how long can we sustain this lead?

- Can the competitive advantage be defended through secrecy (for example through denying source code)?

■   Who else might emerge as a serious competitor, for example through expanding from an adjacent technology, product or market position, and what are the *barriers to entry*?

Having a strong and sustainable competitive advantage is particularly important when trying to enter new markets. It is vital not to underestimate the scale of advantage needed to succeed. It is very difficult to supplant an existing strong supplier, unless one can offer a very large advantage. It is quite common that companies pioneer a new product only to find that a company that is already established in the market just steals the business away through being a fast-follower.

Therefore it is vital to be realistic as well as enthusiastic, and to consider a large number of compelling approaches in order to select ones that have a very high probability of succeeding and of creating sustainable value. It is also essential to have a proper process of project management, risk reduction and technical assurance.

Having spent a lot of time and energy (and cash) on preparing for the business plan through the MARKETS approach to writing a plan, you will now need to pull it together in the best way possible.

Dr Shailendra Vyakarnam is Director of the Centre for Entrepreneurial Learning, Judge Institute of Management, Director of Transitions and Visiting Professor at Nottingham Business School. Further information, e-mail: Shai@transitions.co.uk.

3.2

Market research

Be adventurous in your market research if you do not want your product to flop, says Andy Nairn, planning director at Miles Calcraft Briginshaw Duffy

It's generally estimated that around 90 per cent of new products fail soon after launch. In an attempt to overcome these daunting odds, companies spend huge amounts of time and money researching new ideas with potential customers. But still the success stories are vastly outnumbered by the flops. Why should this be? Ironically, the answer is that many entrepreneurs still take a decidedly unadventurous approach to research.

This section sets out a more imaginative approach to new product research.

START WITH THE RIGHT MINDSET

Too many companies see research as a magic solution to all their problems. And yet the truth is that research can only ever be a tool to assist professionals in making their own judgements. It's an inherently artificial construct which can only hint at the likelihood of success in the real world. As such, it can provide stimulus and insight, clues and guidance – but not answers or decisions and definitely not certainty.

Where companies devolve decision making to their customers they are liable to be misled, and nowhere is this more true than in the field of new product research. For consumers are particularly unreliable when it comes to assessing new concepts – either shying away from anything too radical, getting hung up on details at the expense of the big idea or over-rationalizing their decision making in a way that they would never do in the real world. As Henry Ford observed: 'If I'd asked the public about their transport needs, they would have told me to invent a faster horse.'

The first step to success, then, is to be aware of the limitations of research. Avoid researchers who promise absolute certainty. Read between the lines of respondents' opinions. Most of all, remember that consumers can't make decisions for you: ultimately you will still need to rely on those good old-fashioned qualities, judgement and intuition.

CREATE THE RIGHT CONTEXT

It's ironic that many innovators choose to assess their exciting new ideas in the most dreary settings: clipboard interviews in soulless shopping malls; humdrum focus groups in suburban living rooms; tedious workshops in sterile viewing facilities. Given these uninspiring settings, it's no surprise that good ideas are often crushed while average ones slip through.

Smart innovators ensure that their concepts are explored in an appropriately engaging setting. For instance, if you're dealing with a new food or drink, you might conduct the research in a kitchen or pub; if you're launching a completely new concept, you might give respondents the prototype for a week and observe them using it in their own homes; if you're trying to understand your audience's broader lifestyle, you might give them a camcorder and get them to film a day in their own life.

It will be obvious from the above that there are no right or wrong answers here, but anything that helps contextualize, or even simply enliven affairs will help. In particular, anything that encourages interaction should be considered. Start with the issues needing exploration and ask: what could be done to make this process more interesting, stimulating and relevant?

TALK TO THE RIGHT PEOPLE

All innovators start with high hopes for their product, and many dream of mass-market adoption of their concept before too long. However, it's not always helpful to focus your initial research programme solely on the eventual end-user since, as noted above, the general public is not always the best judge of genuinely new ideas.

Because of this, smart innovators complement their mainstream research programme with conversations with more creative thinkers. These could be people with a special expertise in the marketplace: technical boffins, trade journalists or retail buyers. Alternatively, they could be consumers who are unusually involved in the category: hardcore enthusiasts, heavy users or trend setters. Or they might simply be professionals with a lateral take on the issues: psychologists, sociologists or even anthropologists.

The point here is to balance the (often conservative) reactions of your broader target audience with the (usually more adventurous) attitudes of those 'in the know'. After all, in real life, most new products will only reach the hands of the mass market if they first satisfy the needs of an experimental minority.

THINK DIFFERENT

Most innovation research focuses on whether the new concept is 'better' than its competitors or predecessors. This is all very well (a superior product certainly increases one's chances of success) but ignores a fundamental truth of modern business: that being 'better' doesn't get you very far, for very long, unless you can also stand for something 'different'.

In a world where functional product differences are quickly replicated (and more cheaply) by rival companies, innovators increasingly need to think in terms of enduring brand values: those intangible, emotional qualities which competitors find much harder to duplicate.

So as well all those prototype sketches and rational product descriptions that typify innovation research, you should include plenty of stimuli to help identify the right personality for your concept: alternative names, visual boards to convey mood, video edits which evoke different tones of voice and so on.

Continually remind yourself that while consumers buy products, they buy *into* brands. Otherwise your research programme will simply do the hard work for your competitors, for free.

DON'T LEAVE IT TOO LATE

Finally, innovators should either use research from the start or not at all. If research is brought in at the last minute to overcome doubts, mollify bosses or (frankly) cover backsides then it becomes a costly irrelevance. When it is too late to change anything, when too much time and money has been invested in R&D to turn back, when reputations have been put on the line - proper research can be of very little use, and the pressure to wave through average ideas can be overwhelming.

After all, no amount of research can turn a poor product into a winner. But if innovators adopted a more imaginative approach from the outset, as outlined above, perhaps fewer failures would be progressed in the first place.

Andy Nairn is Planning Director at Miles Calcraft Briginshaw Duffy, one of Britain's leading independent ad agencies. Before this, he spent over ten years at some of the world's top agencies, including Abbott Mead Vickers and Rainey Kelly Campbell Roalfe in London, and Goodby Silverstein in San Francisco. He has worked on a huge range of famous brands, from Virgin Atlantic to Tetley tea. In 2001 he was named one of the top 10 planners in the world, by Campaign *magazine. Contact: tel: 020 7073 6940; email: nairna@mcbd.co.uk*

Brand-based innovation

Innovation based on the brand is the most cost-efficient and effective innovation you will have, says Rita Clifton, Chairman, Interbrand. Just look at Coke, IBM, Intel, Samsung and Tesco

Innovation has become one of Those Words in businesses and organizations of all kinds. It sits alongside 'customer focus', 'openness and transparency' and 'value' as terms that tend to be overused, ill-appreciated and under-delivered. There are a number of factors that conspire to make this the case.

Numerous surveys and correlation studies demonstrate the value and importance of 'innovation' to the most successful enterprises. There is hardly a need to argue the theoretical case any more. The real issue is wrestling down what is really meant by innovation – and how, under all the day-to-day operating and financial pressures, organizations can really sustain the levels of innovation that are required to succeed in every market today and in the future.

WHAT IS INNOVATION?

It is interesting to look at a range of definitions of innovation from marketing textbooks: '*innovation is changing the value and satisfaction obtained from resources by the consumer'*; *'an innovation is an application of ideas and knowledge to meet successfully a current or future market need'*; and, most succinctly, *'invention is a new product, innovation is a new benefit'*. The last definition is also telling in that it distinguishes invention from innovation – something that many organizations find difficult. Producing new 'stuff' – particularly technology – is certainly the most visible and high-profile part. However, there is always a danger that the energy which goes into inventing new products is not focused enough to give the best return on investment – nor to ensure the best minimization of risk. A past president of Coca-Cola went so far as to say *'New products are a lazy man's marketing'*.

The most effective and efficient innovation is brand-based innovation. After all, the brand is the most important and sustainable corporate asset. And indeed, it is usually the most productive asset to sweat. Starting with the brand, and so with the customer insight and relationship, gives a clear and disciplined platform for innovation across the total brand experience, including service, retail/3-D, and in process as well as product areas. It will give longer, deeper and more potentially sustainable competitive advantage than a reliance on product inventions alone – particularly in most of today's markets where long-term product differences are becoming less consumer noticeable.

Strong brands, old or new, have three critical characteristics: clarity, consistency and leadership. That means being clear about what the brand stands for, about its values, its purpose and its future direction, and it means being consistent in living and communicating those clear values, both inside and outside the organization; increasingly, a brand's people are the major part of the brand experience. But the most important characteristic correlating to long-term sustainable value is leadership. This not necessarily about size and financial muscle; it is about 'setting the agenda' and standards in a market, and this can apply as much to brand leaders as to challenger brands. And, above all, it needs great innovation, across all areas of operation.

WHO'S DOING IT WELL?

A good place to start for inspiring examples is among the world's most valuable brands. Coca-Cola is in the pole position it is today not just because they have refreshed and innovated in the product over time. Clearly, Diet Coke, Caffeine-free Coke and Coke with lemon have been important initiatives and 'new news' to retain interest over time, but it was also brand-based thinking about putting Coke's refreshing qualities 'within an arm's reach of desire' that inspired innovation in distribution and merchandising through vending machines. Innovative advertising and marketing communications, including sponsorship, have ensured that the brand stays fresh and current to its young, demanding and otherwise fickle target audiences.

IBM, now No 3 in the world brand league table, may have been kicked into more innovative behaviour by the original product challenge of Apple, but they have made up for it since by innovating and extending the brand around consultancy and e-business. Again, they started not with 'how can we make more and different boxes', but rather 'how can we use our technology, authority and expertise to create more value for our customers?'

Possibly the most intriguing brand in the top 10 is Intel. Clearly, it has helped that Intel is driven by, and lives for, innovation, as it says in its literature, and that it invented the world's first microprocessor. However, what really propelled Intel into its valuable position today was innovation in customer targeting and marketing thinking. Communicating directly with computer buyers, rather than just IT professionals, created real market 'pull', while the Intel Inside cooperative marketing programme ensured that Intel moved from being a technical ingredient to being the ultimate 'cuckoo in the nest' ingredient brand.

Among the many other examples of world-leading brands, Samsung stands out as being the fastest growing out of the top 100 valuable brands. Again, this is not only down to their technical innovation around the digital platform, but also particularly due to their decision to build a premium brand, rather than pursue the low price and commodity, OEM road to perdition. Having made this decision, process innovation came in the form of measuring their people's performance by their contribution to building the value of the Samsung brand as an asset, rather than just being measured by straight financials. It has paid off many times over.

Closer to home, Tesco is probably the best example of a company using brand-based innovation around its customers' 'life needs' to create a constant stream of relevant products, services and marketing initiatives. Its approach to innovation epitomizes the original meaning of the word, derived from the Latin word 'innovare', meaning 'to renew'; Tesco's brand focus on winning lifetime customer loyalty forces a constant state of renewal and growth, and this is championed by the CEO and management team. *Fortune* magazine also had an interesting perspective on this when they described the companies that succeed in innovating as having '*mastered the art of maintaining continuity while fostering a state of perpetual renewal*'.

The word renewal also implies a 'whole company' approach to innovation, and this is still a challenge for so many organizations. While speeches made by CEOs might feature the innovation word, too often innovation is still believed to be the province of the R&D and marketing departments. This leads us into the first point of the last section, which is about the lessons we can draw for more effective and efficient innovation in the future.

SO WHAT?

An innovative culture has to come from the top. This may seem an overused point, but the CEO must be seen as the CBO – ie Chief Brand Officer. The customer focus this brings forces innovation on to everyone's agenda, and encourages people to see the brand as an inspiring – and efficient – central organizing principle for all areas of innovation.

On a parochial note, it would certainly help encourage more innovation from the top if we had a rather more encouraging media climate in the UK. It is a sad but true observation that some UK CEOs are nervous about championing high-profile, unusual innovation in case they are criticized in an increasingly cynical national press. And yet innovation is so critical to the future success and wealth creation in the UK that business leaders must show courage and leadership in taking this on.

You need truly cross-functional and integrated thinking to get the best results. To avoid the 'invention-only'/'not my department' trap, it is critical to include people from across any organization (and absolutely including the finance team) – and to make some type of innovation a measured (and rewarded) part of everyone's roles. It is also critical that this type of working is continuous practice rather than one-off based, and using the brand is a constant source of energy and competitive perspective.

You need true customer obsession. This does not mean commissioning more and more reams of market research; it is just as much to do with looking at macro-trends, behavioural observation and powerful listening to consumers. There are also many and varied participative techniques for getting customer participation in co-creating the future they would like.

Recognize that innovation comes from product, service, 3-D experience or process, and can be breakthrough or incremental... and, above all, use the brand. The brand is not only the major wealth creator in any business; it is also a springboard, a rallying point, and a testing filter for new ideas across the piece. Innovation based on the brand is the most cost efficient and effective innovation you will have.

Finally, of course, there is one thing left to say. If you do not think that your existing brand, or brands, are strong enough to generate the right level and value in innovation... then either renew the brand, or invent a new one. Now, that really is radical, brand-based innovation.

Rita joined Interbrand in 1997 as chief executive and became chairman in 2002. Interbrand Group is the world's leading brand consultancy with offices in over 30 countries. Further information: Interbrand, 85 Strand, London WC2R 0DW. Tel: +44 (0)20 7554 1000; Fax: +44 (0)20 7554 1020.

3.4

Creating difference, provoking reaction

The fortunes of a brand can be transformed by design, argues
Richard Williams of Williams Murray Hamm

People have become hugely media savvy. Possibly as a result of busy, pressurized lives, they filter anything that doesn't interest or engage them. How many posters do you remember from your walk to work today? How many TV ads from last night?

Brand owners, be they in packaged goods or service provision, deliver, by and large, communications that conform to their category. Ads of cars driving down snaky passes are ten a penny, as are fruit juice packs covered in pictures of delicious fruit and instant soup cartons with pictures of mugs on. It's mindless stuff and is mostly the result of fear of failure, over-reliance on market research and a lack of understanding of what's really possible.

While most people involved in marketing understand that different, engaging advertising works better than repetition and intrusion, few have got the message when it comes to design.

There are, of course, notable cases where breaching the category norms and provoking consumer engagement have reaped huge dividends. James Dyson reinvented the vacuum cleaner, getting rid of messy bags, making the machines simple to maintain and designing them to look wonderful – nobody would have taken a second look at a vacuum cleaner before Dyson came along. In the world of FMCG, who would ever have imagined a humble bread wrapper featuring on prime-time TV, as well as taking the glamour slot in one Britain's most popular red tops? Yet this was what happened to Hovis, following its 2002 redesign.

Having struggled for years to broaden its appeal to all types of packaged bread rather than just brown, Hovis took the brave decision to completely reinvent the way the brand was presented. Since it had been around for all of the previous century, you couldn't just change its proposition overnight. Hovis had always been about being good for you (the name derives from 'hominis vis' meaning 'strength of man'), so the brand truth was re-expressed by covering the packs in wholesome toppings, baked beans, cheese, tomatoes, emphasizing that bread is an essential part of the modern diet. Hovis looked and behaved like nothing else on the supermarket shelf and sales leapt, making it the fastest-growing grocery brand in the country in 2002 (TNS).

Not only did the brand grow substantially, but the design is protectable – nobody else in the category can use 'big food'. The creation of intellectual property should be a given for any design project.

Some 'new rules' of branding:

'Old' World	'New' World
About impact, identification	About engagement
Accepts conventions, shared imagery	Totally unique
Execution-based	Ideas-based, 'intellectual property'
Low risk	Higher risk (but high returns)?

CREATING DIFFERENCE

Most businesses simply don't understand the potential that's presented by design. Hovis and, before it, Tango, proved conclusively that the fortunes of brands can be transformed by design, but few businesses, even if they admire these brands, have the infrastructure or even the mindset to do anything but maintain their brands. Huge sums of money are wasted making minor changes that won't resonate with consumers. If you want consumers to see your brand differently, they need to see that it's different.

There are a number of things that companies can do to get more out of design.

Design representation at board level

Few businesses have anybody with responsibility for design at board level, yet they are increasingly placing emphasis upon the value of their brands. Since design is crucial to the success of brands, the lack of senior representation seems a glaring omission. Have someone on the board who understands design and places great value upon it and get them to drive best practice through the company.

Design training

How to buy, evaluate and implement design rarely forms any part of staff training; it's most often learned on live projects which is where the worst habits are picked up. Design businesses themselves will try to inculcate clients by offering free training, but this should be avoided. Formal training programmes should be bought from impartial bodies that represent the design industry and all levels of staff should be subject to these training programmes.

Use of consumer research

Consumer research is often poorly executed and the wrong conclusions drawn. The result of talking to 10 bored housewives in a Surbiton focus group is that you get 10 boring answers and end up responding with boring solutions. There is a better way and that's to use design research to understand your current position, but you should be able to determine your preferred route forward and to evaluate the designs which emerge as a response.

Do not be tempted to let consumers tell you what to do; they aren't clairvoyant and anyway they're not interested enough. Creating the future is what you're paid to do.

If you're anxious, use qualitative research as a disaster check, but balance it with hefty doses of intuition. My rule of thumb is that if it looks right, it's probably wrong, and if it doesn't frighten you then nobody will notice it.

CHOOSING A DESIGN AGENCY

This is very difficult. I'd hate to be a client since so many design agencies seem to offer largely the same thing at roughly the same price. Of course, you must like them enough to want to do business with them, but you must ask yourself what they will add to your project. Pleasant people, particularly good salesmen, are often the most acquiescent people. You will need people who provide you with wise counsel, but know what they are doing and aren't afraid to tell you what to do.

There is no rule of thumb in design. Big agencies are not necessarily better than small ones and expensive ones aren't always better than cheap ones. I would ask them what return on investment their top ten projects have delivered and would always look at their record on creative and effectiveness awards. You might think that awards are just self-congratulatory tosh, but the best designers want to work in agencies where their work will receive acclaim. It's also worthwhile taking up references. Few people do, but a former client can tell what the agency is really like to work with, warts and all.

Further information at www.creatingdifference.com.

3.5

Product launches

Don't shoehorn people into products, says Gareth Ellis at Saatchi & Saatchi, listen to what they want

The challenge for many organizations lies not in being inventive, but mastering innovation. Innovation is the desire to continually explore and test ideas. The restless energy at the heart of innovation sets ideas in motion.

Invention is by its nature more radical and threatening, trying to shatter convention; it is likely to be the idea of one person or a department. Innovation, on the other hand, creates lasting change through continual refinement and iteration, and should be the responsibility of an entire organization.

The difference between Philips and Sony is a case in point. Philips is famous for inventing products, which others successfully innovate. The CD-I was heralded as a games, movie and music player. No one quite knew what it did: it bombed. Sony identified a new gaming audience, refined the concept and launched the PlayStation. The marketing in particular was highly innovative and showed how to escape the gaming ghetto, where gaming was seen as childish, an expression of arrested development.

CD-I's flop is less surprising when you understand that most of Philips' ground-breaking inventions are based on one another; as opposed to careful and reflective listening to what people want. Undoubtedly Philips' light bulb fed the huge demand created by available electricity. However, the valve technology in the light bulb was reapplied to create the radio valve, which in turn inspired the cathode ray tube for TVs. These are extraordinary inventions that should not be devalued; but they do point to transposition by a product-driven organization, not a company that puts the customer at the heart of everything it does.

This is why marketing matters if you want to create an innovative, commercial operation. It's a discipline that centres you on customers. The start point is always trying to understand behaviour and intuit a genuine need. A huge amount is written on how to do this but essentially it comes down to some simple, human skills. Before you can do anything you must learn to listen – and it's amazing how bad organizations are at listening; if you want an innovative culture you must put in place living processes which enable key people to develop these skills.

Once an organization has learnt to listen, they must start to see life from others' point of view. This helps you understand what motivates people, their hopes, fears and dreams. People are constantly refining and adapting the perceptual schema which shapes their experience of the world – and organizations need to do the same. While you can rely on external researchers to do this, it is far better if you develop your own processes which connect you to your customers. By this I do not mean research – a survey or easy telephone call. Go into the field, learn to observe people and develop ways to feed these insights into your customer champions.

This is vital for growth and renewal. If your processes aren't giving you insight into what customers think and feel then you're going to struggle making them happy. These processes are the first step towards becoming market led, fulfilling genuine need as opposed to shoehorning products into people. 3G is a good example of this, where auctioning of bandwidth created a market space, as opposed to a space wanted by the market. It may yet be a great success, but it will continue to flounder until someone identifies an application people want.

PlayStations are successful in a way that Nintendo, Sega and Xbox are not, because they are intrinsic to young people's lives. All these gaming platforms are fun. They all offer a shared social experience. But Nintendo and Sega's positioning has been more childish – from its games graphics to its marketing. Sony wanted to appeal to a much older audience. Their marketing had an underground feel. They launched hoping to be endorsed by alternative culture. Their games were trialled in clubs. Their games were older, darker and more fashion conscious. Doom had an 18 certificate. Wipeout had a soundtrack by punk dance band The Prodigy. ISS Pro featured real football stars and was played obsessively by real football stars.

Brand ambassadors in their early-20s audience created aspirational pull, dragging in young gamers. The original audience is still loyal and in their 30s, while those in their 20s appeal to the next generation of gamers. Innovative marketing enabled PlayStation to develop an alternative reality positioning, The Third Space, vital if your offer connects (mainly young men) to different worlds with simple and understandable rules. We are all heroes on the PlayStation; it is the stuff of dreams. PlayStation still ensures it has grassroots appeal (while Nintendo has had to refocus around hard-core gamers to survive). The PlayStation School's Cup is a football tournament that gives hundreds of schools free professional kits and the chance to play on purpose-built pitches (and, one hopes, escape the telly).

You should never blame your customers for not understanding your product or seeing its value. It is your responsibility to make that connection. Creating interest is hard because of people's innate inertia. This is understandable if you think about the sheer noise overwhelming people each day (3,000 messages by some measures). There are so many brands with the same offering that people look for reasons to discount them. If you want to overcome fatigue – all the reasons not to listen – then you need to introduce a fresh offer in a surprising way.

Word of mouth remains the most effective way of selling: people are much more likely to trust a personal recommendation than a brand's over-promise. You can no longer rely on top-down marcomms to excite people. Advertising still has an important role, but marketers must also stimulate demand from the bottom up, creating excitement within people's own networks.

At the end of the day there's no substitute for a big idea, but it must work across all media in a compelling and coherent way. It must take customers on a journey they will remember. But above all, people must love talking about it.

Saatchi & Saatchi X was created to develop and deliver ideas that inspire loyalty to brands in this new world.

Direct marketing goes interactive

One-to-one dialogue with prospective buyers through multiple channels is close to reality, reports Nik Margolis of Squeeze Digital

In the purest sense, direct marketing defines any promotional activity that seeks to talk directly to the consumer or the buyer as an individual.

Direct marketing is no longer a new medium; in fact, with the advent of digital direct marketing, it's become the foundation upon which many new channels and technologies are based.

In order to understand how powerful digital direct marketing is, particularly in the context of new product launches, it's important to understand how direct marketing has developed over time, and the way direct marketing theory has also developed over the past 30 years.

The first exponents of what became known as direct marketing were the companies who realized that mail could become a retail channel in its own right. Organizations like Reader's Digest paved the way for the sophisticated multi-million-pound industry that exists today. At first the concept appears deceptively simple: build communications that work in print, and mail them out to a prospect base.

In fact, there are obviously a number of other considerations that must go into such a strategy to make it work:

- Make the product look good in print.
- Procure suitable data/postal addresses to which to send the material.
- Develop the appropriate 'back end' operation to handle both the mailing and the response to the mailing.

Over time, many organizations adopted such approaches, and in the 70s and 80s in the UK a highly sophisticated industry began to emerge and take shape, from specialists in the design and production of hard-working mail packs to companies that specialized in the management of the data and the management of the responses; companies which then specialized in the marketing of 'good' data, or 'agencies' that managed the responses more efficiently. Over time, the direct marketing industry grew around the mail channel; as they grew and became more successful, strategists began to specialize in this new form of marketing, and at this point, the first key change in the direction of direct marketing may be noted.

Early adopters of the direct approach were very much focused on the product. How can the product be made to look good? How can we find the right audience for this product? What other products will our customers buy?

As the industry grew, and a greater emphasis was placed on the efficiency of direct marketing spend, questions were asked as to whether the product approach was in fact the best approach. 'Another way' was envisaged, and the first practitioners of what might be understood as 'customer-centric' marketing evolved. Today, most direct marketing is very much of this latter variety. Everything in the direct channel is evaluated against the target audience – instead of asking what products customers will buy, marketers find themselves asking, and indeed, researching, what customers *want* to buy. Creatives toil over research, and work from pen portraits of an audience *before* they consider the product features.

Another key evolution with direct marketing is the increasing rise of the importance of data. Many direct marketers talk about data-driven marketing, and today many of the leading exponents of direct marketing allocate vast resources to highly sophisticated data-driven marketing programmes, such as Tesco's Clubcard programme, the Nectar partnership, highly evolved loyalty programmes such as Air Miles, etc.

The most recent development in direct marketing is the advent of an entirely new channel. It's a channel that appears to bring together the very foundations of direct marketing – the ability to produce messaging which talks directly to a specific audience, and to use data to drive communications. The new channel is often tagged as 'digital', although really there are two elements to this channel, e-mail and 'online'.

The advent of the internet, or more importantly, the rate at which it has been adopted as a tool in the developed world, has changed the direct marketing map. It is estimated that over half the developed world check their e-mail once a day, and in the UK at least, more than three-quarters of people who go online check their e-mail before they do anything else. It is fast becoming an integral part of the channel mix for brands in all aspects of their communication planning, and offers considerable potential for organizations launching new products and services.

UNDERSTANDING CHANNELS IN RESPECT OF PRODUCT LAUNCHES

Planning a launch is probably the most challenging aspect of marketing. This discussion concerns itself solely with some of the channels available within direct marketing and understanding which channels might be suitable for a particular activity. Other elements, such as understanding the right target audience for a product or service, and indeed, researching such an audience in considerable depth, are equally important. Similarly, even if the appropriate channels are known and understood, the content of the messaging and communications developed for those channels, and that audience, are naturally of critical importance.

If we agree that direct marketing is any activity that seeks to talk directly to a prospective consumer or buyer of a product as an individual, there are a huge number of options available to an organization or brand. It's important to extend this definition a little at this point, and consider also those channels and media which, while unable to be truly data driven, or which represent true one-to-one communications, still have the ability to open a personal dialogue with a prospective buyer. Such channels, for example, will include TV advertising, or an outdoor campaign. Advocates of such channels will argue, with justification, that media can now be bought to give a highly articulate degree of one-to-one targeting, but, more importantly, the inclusion within messaging across these channels of a telephone number, e-mail address or website fulfils our requirement to develop one-to-one dialogue.

CHANNEL EVALUATION

Creative impact, relevance and reach

Some channels lend themselves to particular audiences; many factors must be considered when evaluating channels, not least budget, but here I will cover three variables – creative impact, relevance and reach.

It's a common mistake to find one and not all of these considerations factored into a launch plan. The most common mistake is to invest heavily in one channel because it has the greatest reach, to the huge detriment of the relevance. Huge audiences require very broad propositions and messaging, otherwise a large part of that audience will be isolated and ignored by the communications.

Creative impact is a rather broad term to describe the ability of a channel to grip a particular audience and, more importantly, to engage and compel them. By engaging an audience you are doing a lot to compel them to do what you want. Multidimensional channels such as TV or a good rich media website can do a lot for engagement, using high-quality video and audio, or animation, to convey a message with high impact; done in the right way, and to a large extent, combining the messaging with relevance, good creative impact goes a long way to compelling your audience to respond, and to open the all-important dialogue by responding to a specific call to action (for example, 'buy now').

Relevance is one of the founding principles of direct marketing, and depends largely on the channel used. Integrating data into communications is a key driver of relevance. Not simply personalizing a direct mail pack with someone's name, but ensuring (for example) that the contents of that mailpack reflect what is known about that person. Relevance depends on both the channel's inherent ability to drive versionalized communications and the availability of data to support such communications within that channel. For example, TV advertising cannot be versionalized to a great degree, because firstly the technology does not support such delivery (although there are huge advances being made in respect of digital television) and, more importantly, because of the production costs involved with producing different versions of high-quality TV advertisements. Versions of direct mailpacks are somewhat easier to accomplish, and the use of multiple versions of covering letters is something of a marketing chestnut, and a good example of the way in which a channel can accommodate the need for relevance.

Reach concerns the ability of a channel to deliver a message or communications plan to as wide an audience as possible. In most cases, the breadth of the reach available increases the efficiency of the overall spend. But reach must be thought of in terms of target audience, not audience *per se*. While TV as a channel has been discussed above as having good potential in terms of creative impact, it's difficult to buy TV with a highly defined target audience, meaning that the creative impact it is able to deliver must be at a very high level to ensure broad relevance. Again, this can be to the detriment of the relevance of the communications.

Channel by channel

Mail

Table 3.6 (i)   Direct mail as a marketing channel

Creative impact	Relevance	Reach
Medium–high: Mailpacks can deliver extremely impactful creative, and print production techniques today allow for highly unusual and creative formats to be used. Response usually requires a degree of effort from the respondent, either a phone call or the completion of a coupon.	Medium–high: Depending on pack contents, variations driven by data held and targeting can be relatively easy to accommodate. If the creative is good, and engagement is achieved, such relevance can have a considerable bearing on response.	Medium–high: Availability of direct mail lists in both B2B and B2C markets is extensive, and the industry is almost as mature as direct marketing itself. Sophisticated targeting is also available, based not only on actual data held, but also through intelligent data modelling.

TV/iTV

Table 3.6 (ii)   Television as a marketing channel

Creative impact	Relevance	Reach
High:	Low–Medium:	High:
Impact is expensive when using TV, and low production values can be very apparent. Well-produced, polished TV advertising carries high impact, and can be very influential on response, although this is often directly proportional to the ability to target an audience tightly, which can be difficult with broadcast channels.	The nature of TV advertising means that large audiences and reach can be achieved; however, the size of such audiences tends to homogenize their characteristics, meaning the ability to deliver highly targeted and relevant messaging is reduced.	The broadest reach of any of the channels detailed here.

Radio/digital radio

Table 3.6 (iii)   Radio as a marketing channel

Creative impact	Relevance	Reach
Low–Medium:	Medium:	Medium:
Radio is a one-dimensional channel, and while particularly suited to some messaging types (eg retail sales, driving footfall etc), it can be difficult to build dialogue through radio advertising owing to the fact that a substantial part of the audience may be in their cars and therefore unable to respond, and lacks impact when compared to more visual channels.	The advent of digital radio, and the extensive network of private and regional programming in many countries means it is possible to find specific program audience profiles which match a brief. Versionalization is generally not feasible or practical.	A sophisticated network of stations, with sizeable audiences exists in most developed countries, and depending on the proposition and audience being targeted, radio can represent a viable route to a particular audience.

Websites

Table 3.6 (iv)   Websites as a marketing channel

Creative impact	Relevance	Reach
High: In recent years, the advancement in the technology behind digital technology means that websites can carry as much creative impact as TV advertising; the ability to offer interaction within a website means that a higher degree of creativity and impact can be delivered.	Medium: The relevance of website communications often depends on the methods through which traffic is generated. It's possible and, in terms of budget, highly feasible to deliver traffic into versions of a site depending on source, eg customers may be fed through to a customer site, while prospects go to a slightly different version. Similarly, real-time data capture can personalize the experience of a site visit 'on the fly', adding to the relevance.	Medium–high: Across the developed world 'most' people now have internet access; certain technologies can limit accessibility and thereby reach, and bandwidth should always be a consideration of site designers in respect of the anticipated audience visiting the site. It should be recognized that the reach of a website is not in fact deliverable by the website itself; such traffic must be generated through other activities, such as online advertising, or e-mail.

E-mail

Table 3.6 (v) E-mail as a marketing channel

Creative impact	Relevance	Reach
High:	High:	Low–medium:
E-mail marketing is developing into a highly sophisticated direct marketing industry in its own right. It's now possible to deliver rich media within an e-mail message, and HTML is no longer defined as formatted text and pictures. Instead, it's a highly creative channel, much like press or TV advertising. Respect must be paid to the fact that of all the channels listed here (with the exception of SMS marketing) it's the most invasive, but still carries a high degree of creativity.	It's possible to drive the content of an e-mail from a database. Provided the initial template is designed to accommodate such a dynamic population, relevance can be assured in this way. The greater the required degree of relevance, the more resource is required to create the communications, as all content variables must be prepared and created to conduct the campaign.	The relatively high transience of e-mail addresses, and increasing sophistication of spam filters and federal laws restricting non-permission-based e-mail marketing, means that in most countries the availability of good quality e-mail data is fairly limited. Strategies that collect targeted data at source, however, are highly viable, and worthy of consideration in respect of product launches.

Telephone

Table 3.6 (vi)   Telemarketing as a marketing channel

Creative impact	Relevance	Reach
Low: It's difficult to inject creativity and impact into a telemarketing programme. The general reception of outbound telemarketing is also fairly low (perhaps higher in respect of B2B telemarketing). Good quality inbound call handling can deliver a degree of impact, particularly in respect of the relatively low expectations most consumers have of the channel itself.	High: Telemarketing can be integrated well with data held as, ultimately, it is the truest representation of one-to-one dialogue. Good call scripting and, more importantly, high quality, truly empowered telemarketers can bring data into a call script and maximize the potential afforded by the contact.	Medium–high: In pure terms the reach of telemarketing is high, as the availability of good clean lists is also relatively high; however, it's an expensive medium and, depending on the audience, the reach can be affected by inefficiency, particularly with certain audience groups, eg high-value or senior B2B decision makers.

Channel integration

When considering channels for any campaign, including new product or service launches, integration across different channels can have a substantial impact upon response, compared to channels working in isolation. The typical example cited is often direct mail followed by telemarketing, where the mailpack serves to put the brand or product in the mind of the recipient, 'warming them up' to the telemarketing.

I have had similar success in respect of digital channels working with telemarketing. An initial telephone call preceding the deployment of an e-mail works well, with the recipient being asked to give permission for the e-mail to be sent. The telemarketer is then notified in real time when the e-mail is opened, and is able to track any activity as a result, for example the respondent clicking through to a website, and may opt to make further contact at that time. The recipient is usually relatively warm to the call at this point and both contact and conversion rates are higher than traditional 'cold' telemarketing, introducing increased efficiency through the integration of two channels.

There are also natural partners – as digital becomes a more accepted part of the marketing mix, it is unusual to find any communications strategy, particularly product launches, which ignores the use of e-mail and websites. As noted in the channel comparisons above, a combination of e-mail and website work can give high impact, high relevance and high reach, and in my opinion must form a key part of any communication strategy.

GETTING YOUR PROPOSITION RIGHT

Alongside channel selection, the proposition is the key consideration when planning and executing the launch of a new product or service. The proposition is exactly what we wish to push forward to a selection of known individuals that is going to engender the desired response. It's important to think with enormous clarity when considering your proposition. It's also essential to consider the characteristics of the individuals that comprise your recipients, as different audiences will require different propositions. The great benefit of direct marketing is the ability to segment your audience, and target different groups of individuals by using the data held to present them with different propositions.

The point here is that direct marketing offers sufficient sophistication to deliver very specific propositions to the right audience, yet it's often overlooked. How often do we see new products and services being launched which we ourselves might consider but which fail to tick an important box on our checklist? I receive e-mail marketing more and more these days, but precious little seeks to talk to me as an individual. Many established brands market to their best customers in the same way in which they market to everybody – they fail to consider what they already know about each customer and so they fail to take advantage of what this data would tell them about what motivates each one to buy.

When planning messaging, it's important to define a list of key audience groups and their characteristics to develop relevant propositions for each. When actually writing your propositions, you need to ask the following questions of each:

- Does it say why the prospect should buy your product?
- Does it clearly state the primary benefit of your product?
- Is it single minded?

If it meets these criteria, it's a proposition that can be worked with. Don't set out to write a headline, but bear in mind that some of the best propositions often end up as such.

A proposition is like a favourite T-shirt. If it looks good, you want it, but you're not going to buy it if it doesn't fit you, and fit you well.

Every launch is different, and the importance of testing cannot be overstated. It should not be limited to channels or propositions but also other key variables such as data selection or media planning. Similarly, realistic benchmarks must be agreed in advance of any activity, and these must be measured over an agreed period before any terminal or conclusive decision is made as to performance.

The flexibility of digital channels, in terms of their ability to deliver data-driven communications of high relevance and creative impact, means that it should be a highly regarded option for the launch of a new product or service. It's a most immediate channel, and response can be gathered and analysed in real time, meaning that it has a very useful ability to deliver both clear and early learning about your communication strategy. As the adoption of the internet as a communication channel continues to grow, this learning can serve an organization well, and the channel itself will continue to deliver good results across the customer base as a whole.

Launched on 1 September 2004, Squeeze Digital is the new digital direct marketing agency specializing in highly creative, data-driven and intelligently managed direct digital marketing. Founded by award-winning marketers and equipped with its own technology platform, Squeeze Digital offers the ultimate in strategic planning, creative development and campaign management. Squeeze Digital works across all digital direct marketing media, including e-mail, microsites, websites and online advertising.

Nik Margolis is a career direct and digital marketing professional who has spent over 10 years working for two of the country's top five direct marketing agencies. More recently Nik has founded Squeeze Digital, the country's leading creatively driven digital direct marketing agency.

Nik's experience covers traditional direct marketing, digital channels and contact centres, and he has worked for some of the biggest brands, including Barclaycard, RM, Volkswagen, BMW, Sky, NTL and the BBC.

A regular platform speaker, Nik has presented at industry conferences on behalf of the Institute of Direct Marketing, and is a regular contributor to the marketing press.

Further information:
www.squeezedigital.com

3.7

Multiple channels

How do you communicate with consumers who are media rich but time poor, asks Ben Wood at MCBD

Twenty years ago, ten years ago even, planning the communications path between a brand and its target audience was a relatively straightforward process. There was only one commercial TV station – commanding huge audiences (at least until the launch of Channel 4 in November 1982). There were for a long time no commercial radio stations (the first was LBC and Capital Radio in 1973). The weekend papers were just that – not a library of magazines and CDs. There were only a clutch of consumer magazines (and the notion of a celebrity weekly would have been laughed out of Emap). Cinema multiplexes were only a twinkle in Branson's eye, poster sites came in standard sizes, and the internet, mobile phones and the wealth of what is now termed ambient media simply did not exist.

Brands could reach huge numbers of people through a single TV spot. Standout in other media channels was straightforward and unchallenging.

Things have changed, and the modern brand has to work very much harder to communicate and, more importantly, motivate consumers. This chapter seeks to outline the explosion of the communication channels that sit between brands and consumers and understand the implications to the modern advertiser.

THE EXPLOSION OF CHOICE

Depending on which report you believe, consumers are currently bombarded with somewhere between 3,000 and 5,000 commercial messages a week. That's a lot of advertising, across a wealth of different channels.

An interesting exercise is to think about your own media consumption across a typical working day in your life, perhaps even keep a diary. It might have started with the radio in the shower and a flick through the paper with breakfast, taken in poster advertising on the way into work (via roadside in the car or cross-track on the train), seen you surfing the net mid-morning and taking in more posters or perhaps bus sides when popping out to get a sandwich at lunch. The afternoon might have seen you staring at seat adverts in a taxi on the way to a meeting, then more outdoor on the way home and probably some television and perhaps some more radio in the evening. And that's just the above-the-line advertising!

It's also likely that you will have encountered a wealth of point of sale (from shelf wobblers to hanging mobiles) and maybe some ambient advertising (sandwich bags or pavement stickers, for example). You will no doubt have received DM through your door or into your e-mail inbox and perhaps had SMS messages zapping into your phone. You might have even been invited to sample products in store, attended a brand-orientated event or been approached by hit squads out on the street.

The list is endless, but the implication is clear: there are more and more ways for brands to connect with consumers every day. And it's not just new channels – traditional channels are fragmenting and proliferating. There are now over 500 television channels available in the UK, new magazines are launched every month, radio is set to boom with the spread of digital sets across the UK and innovation in outdoor sees new shapes and sizes launched every year. You get the picture.

THE COMMUNICATIONS CHALLENGE

It seems that rather than entrenching into set behavioural patterns and sticking with only a selection of favourite channels, consumers are embracing this new media landscape and becoming incredibly savvy in their consumption habits, dipping in and out of channels as they choose. Consumers are now media rich but time poor and it is essential to bear this in mind when developing a communications plan for any brand.

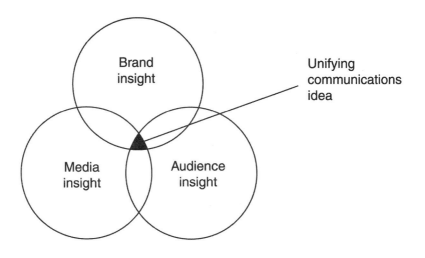

Figure 3.7: *Media Connections must be relevant and motivating*

As a result, the notion of the traditional mass-market media delivery channel is becoming outmoded – the ITV share of all TV viewing is currently dipping towards the 50 per cent mark for the first time, for example.

This is increasingly problematic for brands as they seek to communicate with groups of target consumers. Fragmentation and proliferation mean that old-fashioned interruption marketing becomes less and less relevant. The 30-second TV spot is no longer the universal panacea.

Instead of simply bombarding consumers with advertising communication across the many channels available, brands need now to understand how to connect with consumers in a relevant and motivating way, across all the possible touch points.

A true connection is only possible for brands that approach their communications planning with a driving idea that unites the audience, the brand and the medium. The idea must be king, and not simply the channel for that idea.

This approach is not about allocating 5 per cent of a brand's spend into clever stunts and reserving the remaining 95 per cent for the more traditional approach of whacking creative work out in the most relevant channels and hoping frequency will drive the message home. This is about uniting disciplines and developing a big idea, and increasingly, it's only with that big idea that brands will be able to connect with their target consumers.

A great example is the Stella Artois involvement in film; this has seen a communications plan span movie screenings in unusual locations, a dedicated Stella screen web presence and the sponsorship of quality films on Channel 4.

This approach assumes a utopia of idea-centric orientation within the client company as well as its agencies. But is it really possible?

MEDIA-NEUTRAL PLANNING AS A DISCIPLINE

To unite brand, audience and media insight and develop true idea-centric communications plans requires a totally neutral approach.

Marketers and their agencies really must start the process with a blank piece of paper and with no preconceived ideas about what might or might not be the correct approach. Campaign planning should start from the view that no one medium/discipline has a greater chance of being selected than any other.

The problem is (potentially) that no one agency or client is capable of this alone. Media-neutral planning is, as Simon Marquis, the chairman of Zenith Optimedia, puts it, the 'holy grail' of advertising. 'Communications ecstasy.'

WHO IS BEST PLACED TO OFFER MEDIA-NEUTRAL PLANNING ADVICE?

Creative agencies have been busy hiring media-neutral communications planners to try to deliver against this requirement but there is a problem in that these agencies (traditionally the home of the brand) are still perceived by many to have a natural inclination towards lovingly crafted TV adverts and at best an inclination towards above-the-line solutions. As Kelly Clark, the chief executive of Mindshare, was quoted as saying in *Campaign*: 'Understanding media channels will always be secondary (at creative agencies) to investing in creative talent and producing big budget advertising campaigns.'

On the other side of the fence, media agencies have been quick to try to establish themselves as neutral planning shops; however, there are problems on this side too, with complex buying deals with media owners often muddying the waters. Many feel that it's difficult to deliver true media-neutral solutions with one hand when looking to hit deal targets with the other.

Clearly the above are sweeping generalizations but the point remains that creative and media agencies alone are possibly not the best source of media-neutral advice.

Coming closest currently are the new wave of specialist brand-orientated communications planning shops such as Naked, Rise and Michaelides and Bednash. By separating themselves out from both creative and media agencies and by employing both brand and media specialists they aim to offer the most neutral advice in the market – and currently they probably succeed.

In my mind, however, these agencies feel annexed and represent yet another link in the chain between brand and consumer – surely the key to success is the notion of total integration, and not just between agencies but also with the brand marketing team.

As Jonathan Durden, the chairman of PHD group, predicts: 'I believe that a new superbreed of thinking talent should sit at the heart of each of the marketing networks. Instead of every single company trying to replicate everybody else, it should be cleaned up and resourced at the centre.'

Ben Wood is media director at MCBD, one of only a handful of advertising agencies to offer clients fully integrated strategic media thinking, with its media department sitting alongside both the above-the-line offering and the new through-the-line offering, Elvis.

By placing media planning at the heart of the process, the agency is well placed to offer its clients totally media-neutral solutions, born of both consumer and brand insights that are fully integrated into the creative idea.

The media team works across a base of about half the agency's clients, billing over £10,000,000. Key clients include Thorntons, BT Syntegra, BBC Magazines, Kwik Save, Marshall Cavendish, Viatel and Hollywood Bowl.

The agency works alongside a number of the largest media planning and buying agencies in the business (from PHD and Carat to McCann's and Starcom) to help implement its communication strategies.

Appendix

Living innovation feedback form

We would really appreciate your feedback on this year's 2004 event. We will use your feedback to improve future events and other services offered by the DTI.

1. Venue attended:

2. What action has tonight's event prompted you to take?
   - ❏ Develop new/improved products
   - ❏ Develop new/improved services
   - ❏ Develop a new business model
   - ❏ Improve internal processes
   - ❏ Eliminate waste
   - ❏ Acquire new technology
   - ❏ No action
   - ❏ Other. Please specify:

3. What do you see as the main barriers to innovation?
   - ❏ No major barriers
   - ❏ Access to finance for growth
   - ❏ Access to new technologies
   - ❏ Knowledge of potential markets

- ❏ Planning regulations and law
- ❏ Company regulations and law
- ❏ Skills shortages
- ❏ Other. Please specify:

4. Which of the following DTI new business support solutions do you intend to apply for?

- ❏ Succeeding Though Innovation
- ❏ Small Firms Loan Guarantee
- ❏ Achieving Best Practice in Your Business
- ❏ Selective Finance for Investment (England only)
- ❏ None of the above

5. Which of the following DTI innovation-related publications have you read?

- ❏ The Innovation Report
- ❏ The 2003 R&D Scoreboard
- ❏ The 2003 Value Added Scoreboard
- ❏ Standards and Intellectual Property Rights – a guide to DTI business support for innovation
- ❏ 'Succeeding Through Innovation' – a guide to DTI business support for innovation
- ❏ Creating Value from Your Intangible Assets
- ❏ Critical Success Factors – an intangible assets self-assessment tool for business
- ❏ None of the above

6. Would you take part in an e-mail survey to provide an innovation performance evaluation?

- ❏ No
- ❏ Yes. If yes, please provide your e-mail address below

Index

NB: page numbers in *italic* indicate figures or tables